Prediction Markets Supporting Technology Assessment

Cédric Gaspoz

Cédric Gaspoz

Prediction Markets Supporting Technology Assessment

Corporate applications of prediction markets to support decision making

Lausanne - Switzerland — Vancouver - Canada — 2011

Cédric Gaspoz, PhD

For more information on this topic visit the author's website. You can also download an electronic version or the source files of this book from the website.

E-mail: cedric@gaspoz-fleiner.com
Web: http://cedricgaspoz.com

This book won Cédric Gaspoz the prestigious *"Prix de la Solidarité Confédérale 2011"* award for the excellence of his doctoral thesis, in November 2011.

ISBN 1-468-05403-1

Front cover illustration: Andrey Prokhorov
Back cover photograph: Jean-Sébastien Monzani

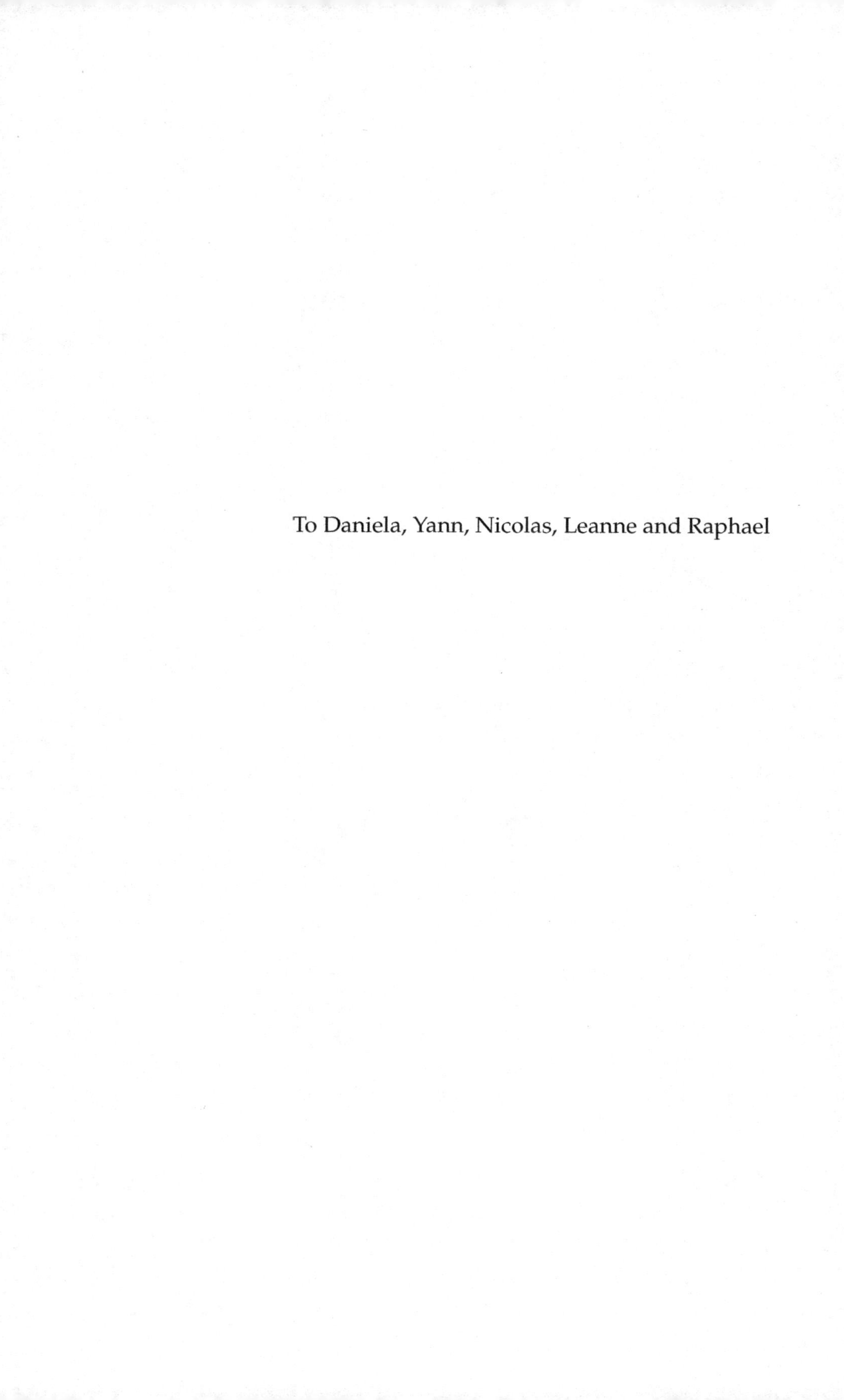

To Daniela, Yann, Nicolas, Leanne and Raphael

Acknowledgements

I would like to write a few lines to thank all the people who supported me in the completion of this research. Because of them, the difficult moments were easier to overcome.

Foremost, I would like to sincerely thank my PhD thesis advisor Prof. Yves Pigneur without whom I would not have been able write this book. He has been a wonderful mentor, always present and ready to help whenever I needed him. During moments of uncertainty, he unfailingly found the right way to guide me through this challenging journey.

As well, I want to express my profound gratitude to my thesis jury composed of Prof. Shirley Gregor, Jean-Fabrice Lebraty and François Grize for their comments and input.

I also want to thank all my colleagues and friends from HEC Lausanne, the Information Systems Institute and the PhDnet for the great time spent together and then to thank the Infocentre team for their great support during my thesis, and in particular Luis Rodriguez for providing me all the necessary infrastructure to develop and run my experiments.

Moreover, I want to particularly thank my colleagues Jan, Jean-Sé, Amine, Delphine and Boris who shared my office during these years.

Furthermore, I would like to thank my copy-editor, Paul Beverley, who did a good job of catching all my mistakes and helping to improve the overall quality of the manuscript.

Of course, I would like to warmly thank my parents for their unconditional support during the hardest moments of my studies.

Finally, my most sincere gratefulness to my spouse Daniela and our children Yann, Nicolas, Leanne and Raphael, who progressively shared my life during the ups and downs of these past years. I really appreciated Daniela's love, support, unlimited patience and understanding. Without her, it would have been much more difficult to produce this thesis.

Contents

Acronyms

AAI	Authentication and authorization infrastructure
AMEX	American Stock Exchange
BSD	Berkeley Software Distribution
CDA	Continuous double auction
CDAwMM	Continuous double auction with a market maker
CEO	Chief executive officer
CERN	European Organization for Nuclear Research
CFTC	Commodity Futures Trading Commission
CVS	Concurrent versions system
DJIA	Dow Jones Industrial Average
DPM	Dynamic pari-mutuel
DS	Design science
DSR	Design science research
DSRM	Design science research methodology
DSS	Decision support system
ECV	Expected commercial value
EPFL	Swiss Federal Institute of Technology in Lausanne
FIFA	International Federation of Association Football
FX	Foresight Exchange
GDSS	Group decision support system
GPL	GNU public licence
GPRS	General packet radio service
GSM	Global system for mobile communications
HSX	Hollywood Stock Exchange
HTML	HyperText markup language
IAM	Information aggregation mechanism
IDE	Integrated development environment
IEM	Iowa Electronic Market

IF	Idea Futures markets
IOC	International Olympic Committee
IPO	Initial public offering
IS	Information systems
ISDR	Information systems design research
ISDT	Information systems design theory
IT	Information technology
LDAP	Lightweight directory access protocol
MBA	Master of business administration
MCDM	Multi-criteria decision-making
MICS	Mobile information and communication systems
MIT	Massachusetts Institute of Technology
MScBIS	Master of science in business information systems
MSR	Market scoring rules
NCCR	National Centre of Competence in Research
NFC	Near field communication
NFL	National Football League
NPD	New product development
NPV	Net present value
NSS	Negotiation support systems
NYSE	New York Stock Exchange
PAM	Policy analysis market
PAN	Personal area network
PDA	Personal digital assistant
PM	Prediction market
RFC	Request for comments
RFID	Radio-frequency identification
ROI	Return on investment
SLF	Swiss Federal Institute for Forest, Snow and Landscape Research
SMI	Swiss market index
SMS	Short message service
SNSF	Swiss National Science Foundation
SPEx	Scientific prediction exchanges
SPRT	Sequential probability ratio test
STOC	Securities trading of concepts

SVN	Apache Subversion
SWX	Swiss Exchange
TFA	Technology futures analysis
ULB	Ultra low band
UNIL	University of Lausanne
VSM	Virtual stock markets
VWAP	Volume weighted average price
WAN	Wide area network
WAP	Wireless application protocol
WSM	Weighted sum model

Part I.

Background and Motivation

1. Introduction

1.1. Background and Research Context

The research presented in this book was part of the National Centre of Competence in Research "Mobile Information and Communication Systems" (NCCR MICS) sponsored by the Swiss National Science Foundation (SNSF). The project is tackling all the technological challenges that have to be addressed in order for wireless sensor networks to realize their full potential, from the study of fundamental principles to the development of platforms, and to their deployment in applications (mainly in the environmental area).

This research was part of the "In-network information management" project. Its main objective was to design and operate a prediction market to assess technological projects running under NCCR MICS. Emerging in 2005, prediction markets had no real implementations in this context. Prediction markets are using the tools and methods for trading commodity and financial futures to predict the outcome of future events. Such electronic markets, trading on claims concerning political events or sports results, have proven to be an accurate predictor of future events, and should have applications to technology foresight and R&D portfolio management.

We decided to follow two tracks to achieve this research. The first one is to evaluate the possibility of using prediction markets for R&D portfolio management. This involves designing, running and evaluating prediction markets in various contexts given that it is almost impossible to evaluate them in a real R&D context. This is so mainly because, in order to evaluate their ability to correctly balance R&D portfolios in a real context, this research should have been run during the whole R&D process, i.e. a decade, from the project idea to the commercialization. So we chose various related contexts to develop and test our designs and then made a theoretical evaluation of our model.

The second track is to compare prediction markets to another technological forecasting method to evaluate the efficiency and the accuracy of prediction markets in such a setup. For this part, we were able to run a prediction market based on the claims produced by previous multi-criteria decision-making (MCDM) experiment on mobile payment. This will support our assumption that prediction markets are good at solving such issues and, furthermore, will help us conclude that prediction markets are an appropriate tool for R&D portfolio management, given their ability to correctly assess new technological projects.

1.2. Relevance and Research Objective

In industry or in universities, it is still very difficult to evaluate, choose and pursue the "right" projects. By right, we understand the projects that will bring the most payback in terms of revenue, image, results or recognition as defined in the organization's strategy. This is even more difficult for technological projects, whose life could be very short due to a rapid turnover.

Our research assumption is that a specifically designed prediction market could improve the R&D portfolio management process. In our context, prediction markets are future electronics markets concerning the potential projects of the portfolio. Prediction markets collect information coming from different actors, who trade on the market, and then aggregate this information at an automatically negotiated equilibrium price corresponding to the valuation of the project. All actors directly or indirectly linked to the project can trade (buy or sell) contracts concerning the projects, based on their own appreciation of the project. The traders are both the leaders and teams of the project, and also the senior management, people from marketing, finance and all the other businesses units concerned with R&D. Their specialized expertise of a particular company activity, such as research – but also marketing, sales, customer care or finance – will enable them to build their own opinion about the project, from the particular viewpoint of their activity field. The result of all aggregated appreciations will de facto include a multitude of implicit criteria related to all company activities.

In addition, prediction markets are very powerful tools for discovering and aggregating the information shared between many people. Thus, using prediction markets should not only make the whole process more effective, but also increase the quality of the decisions, based on information that is more comprehensive.

Our approach is based on the intuition that the information needed to manage the portfolios is generally available within the company in a subjective form. Also prediction markets are able to discover and incorporate this information without the need for quantifying these data through a resource-intensive process.

Consequently, supported by a prediction market artifact, managers should be able to make their decisions in a faster way, while being better informed. Therefore we will evaluate the relevance of our research assumption in three ways: global process improvement (wider participation, effective data collection and user-friendliness of the method), better data accuracy (accurate and up-to-date data) and increased quality of decisions. These evaluations will be made during the testing of our different prototypes and will be completed by interviews with decision makers involved in the process.

Our research question is to demonstrate that specifically designed prediction markets are able to efficiently solve complex technological forecasting issues. This implies studying the design principles of these prediction markets, their adequacy for solving complex claims and their efficiency compared to other tools.

Based on this research question, our research objective is to design a prediction market to support the assessment of new technologies, particularly from the R&D portfolio management perspective. During this research, we will iteratively design, build and evaluate an information technology (IT) artifact in various contexts to study the design factors, the underlying process and the efficiency of these markets.

1.3. Rigor and Theoretical Frameworks

Our work takes place at the intersection of three research domains: technology management, market theories and crowd motivation.

1.3.1. Technology management

Technology management embraces a whole range of concepts such as R&D management, innovation, assessment of new technologies, etc. There are some attempts to structure technology management based on a process approach [61], resulting in a process-based technology management framework. In our case, we chose to use and improve the Levary and Han technological forecasting framework [101].

1.3.2. Market theories

Hayek's hypothesis [83] and Fama's efficient market hypothesis [45] are the foundations of the whole prediction markets literature. There are a lot of publications related to the market mechanisms of prediction markets. This includes information gathering, information aggregation, manipulations, etc. Kambil and van Heck [89] studied electronic markets from the MIS point of view. They identified ten distinct processes that support exchange relations. Moreover, they proposed a stakeholder-process analysis framework for comparing different instantiations of markets.

1.3.3. Crowd motivation

Titmuss's hypothesis that monetary compensation tends to undermine civic duty [164] has been recently "rediscovered" and numerous studies examined the effects of monetary rewards on motivation. Frey and Oberholzer-Gee [49] developed a new framework to study the crowding out of intrinsic motivation when price incentives are introduced. They tend to bridge the gap between econometric and social psychology research on motivation. Recently, Roberts and al. [139] published a new framework to study the motivation of crowds participating in open-source software (OSS) projects.

These three domains can be used solely or in combination to answer our research question. The technology management perspective will help us understand the needs of firms regarding their competitiveness and their sustainability as well as their foresight expectations. The market perspective will help us to understand why prediction markets are so successful in efficiently aggregating dispersed information and how to design them. Finally, the crowd motivation perspective will help us to understand the motivations of traders sharing information with the platform and how to strengthen their involvement in the overall process.

In this book, we mostly focus on technology management and market efficiency. An extensive literature review on prediction markets is presented in chapter 2. Technology management is introduced in chapters 6 and 7.

1.4. Research Approach and Methodology

As stated in the previous section, we will not be able to follow new technology projects from start to finish, mainly because of the length of the overall process, which exceeds the timeframe of this research.

So in order to test our assumptions, we decided to tackle the problem from a number of perspectives. These perspectives are the design factors of a prediction market, their ability to support a given part of the R&D portfolio management process and their ability to operate more efficiently than other technological forecasting methods.

To address these issues, we chose to follow an iterative approach, allowing us to test our design in a specific context, evaluate it and build the results into the next prototype. The most suitable research paradigm in this context is indubitably the design science one. Hevner et al. propose a design science research framework for information systems research. We will use their approach, as illustrated in Figure 1.1, focusing on the build–evaluate loop, to conduct our research. These iterations enable us to build and assess an artifact, before its being refined and reassessed.

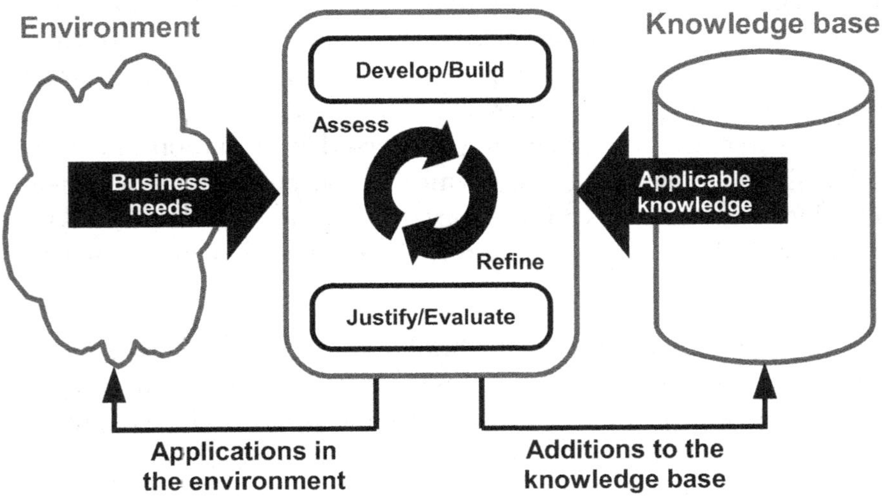

Figure 1.1.: Information systems research framework, according to Hevner et al.

In order to build our artifact, following the Hevner et al. framework, we started examining the relevance of our research, interviewing researchers in the NCCR-MICS projects but also reviewing some literature on R&D portfolio management, enabling us to identify the main business needs. We then made an extensive literature survey on prediction markets to identify and apply the current knowledge to our artifact, ensuring the rigor of our research.

We then started our three iterations in various contexts, building and evaluating our artifact as presented in part III of this book. These multiple evaluations and refinements led us formulate our contributions to both the environment and the knowledge base.

1.5. Contributions

Our research aims to provide multiple theoretical and practical contributions. These will be presented in a more detailed way in chapter 8 but are briefly summarized in this section.

1.5.1. Managerial contributions

Five prediction markets design propositions

The application of prediction markets for technology foresight requires careful choice of design for the artifact. Based on our evaluations of various experiments, we summarized our findings in five propositions for running prediction markets in a technology assessment context.

R&D portfolio management process supported by prediction markets

In order to tackle three main issues encountered in the R&D portfolio management process, i.e. (1) selecting the right criteria, (2) collecting the data, (3) and negotiating the portfolio between the different stakeholders, we propose a new process, aided by a prediction market. We also develop a roadmap to implement it in companies.

1.5.2. Methodological contributions

Technology foresight comparison framework

In the process of benchmarking our technology foresight methods, we developed a comparison framework for such methods. This allows us to better understand the relations between the context in which the assessment is done and the requirements of the artifact in this same context.

1.5.3. Theoretical contributions

Typology to support the design of prediction markets

Resulting from our literature review and our first experiment, we developed an exhaustive typology of design factors to support the construction of prediction market artifacts. These factors could be combined to address specific assessment needs. We also provide prediction market settings for three different contexts based on this typology.

IPO process for prediction markets

Technology foresight being a continuous process, we had to develop a way for participants to submit or propose new ideas. We therefore developed an IPO process to support the creation and the evaluation of new ideas (projects or technologies) without the need for a human review process.

1.6. Structure of the Book

Starting with chapter 2 we present the prediction market approach to forecast uncertainty. This extensive literature review helps us to understand the global environment of prediction markets and also provide a major contribution to the knowledge needed for ensuring the rigor of the following chapters.

Chapter 3 presents the methodology we used to pursue our research objectives. Beside an introduction to design science, we also present our design process.

Chapter 4 is the starting point of our design work on the artifact. We first identified the business needs and the general requirements, before defining the main design factors. We finally built the first artifact, the MarMix prototype.

Chapters 5–7 are the results of three subsequent iterations. The first iteration, presented in chapter 5, presents our multiple experiments of prediction markets as collective forecasting tools in various contexts. This chapter led us to discover the main issues using prediction markets in our particular context and enable us to formulate our design propositions.

Chapter 6 builds on the results from chapter 5 and proposes a new prediction market supported R&D portfolio management process. We start by presenting the relevance of our approach and then, describe the theory we will use to build our artifact, we establish the foundations of our approach. We finish by presenting a proposal to run prediction markets to support this process and drafting a roadmap for stakeholders.

Chapter 7 is the final step in our design process. Building on our findings, we design and run a prediction market for technological forecasting. To achieve this goal, we made a benchmark between a prediction market and an MCDM process. In order to assess the strength of both approaches, we developed a comparison framework for technological forecasting methods. Finally we determined the key success factors of both methods.

Finally, chapter 8 summarizes our research process using the guidelines from Hevner et al. and presents our contributions, supported by Gregor's Information Systems Design Theory. We also discuss some final thoughts about what has been accomplished and what could be done for further research.

2. Using markets to forecast uncertainty

In this chapter, we start by presenting an extensive review of the prediction markets literature, giving the reader a strong understanding of this area, and conclude with the presentation of three open problems of interest to us that will be addressed in the rest of this book.

2.1. Introduction

In August 2004, Google raised $1.4 billion for its IPO. For the first time, Google used an auction mechanism to define its IPO price. However, the IPO price was 15.3% under the first-day market capitalization. This resulted in a waste of $350 million for Google. At the same time, Joyce Berg from the University of Iowa was experimenting with a prediction market "to forecast the market capitalization of Google at the close of the first day of trading"[17]. Iowa's prediction market was only 4% over it. This could have saved Google $225 million.

The underlying idea of prediction markets is based on Hayek's hypothesis [83] and the efficient market hypothesis [45]. In his critiques of central planning in democracy, Hayek claims that in competitive markets the information scattered among all participants is efficiently aggregated in the price function. Furthermore, Fama [45] found that in an efficient market, each new available piece of information is instantly incorporated into the price of a security. Thus, the current price of a security represents the traders' expectation about the future value of the underlying product.

Built on these findings, prediction markets use the same concepts to predict the outcome of uncertain future events. The securities are linked to future events, and the value of the securities represents the aggregated expectation of the traders regarding the outcome of the event.

To illustrate the functioning of a prediction market, we will take a current outcome from the Foresight Exchange as an example. The "Claim Terr10 – Another US Terrorist < 2010" aims at predicting the supervening of a terrorist attack against the USA before 1/1/2010.

> "After Sept. 15, 2001 and before 1/1/2011, official US government sources will claim (in reference to events occurring after Sept. 15, 2001) that a major act or set of connected acts of terrorism, war, crime or rebellion has resulted in at least 200 human deaths in the United States within some 48 hour period. The U.S. government sources must clearly claim that the deaths involve use of deadly force with intent which originated outside official U.S. government channels".

In this case, this "Claim Terr10 – Another US Terrorist < 2011" share will pay the following:

$$\begin{cases} \$100 \text{ if an attack occurs before 1/1/2011;} \\ \$0 \text{ otherwise.} \end{cases}$$

The price p of the security represents the expected payoff, assuming the fact that we are in an efficient market. If T represents a terrorist attack against the USA, and $\Pr(T)$ the probability that an attack occurs before 1/1/2011, then the price p would be:

$$p = \Pr(T) \times 100 + [1 - \Pr(T)] \times 0$$

At any given time, we can derive $\Pr(T)$ from p, which represents the consensus among the traders regarding the probability that an attack will occur before 1/1/2011.

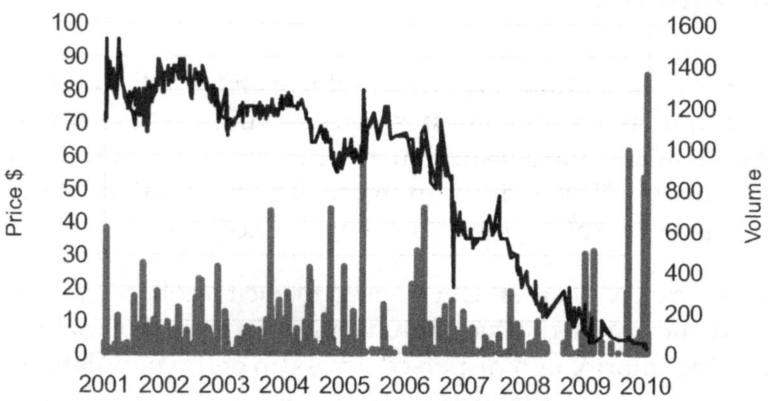

Figure 2.1.: Variation of "Claim Terr10" price on Foresight Exchange

As presented in Figure 2.1, the price for the share was \$4. This means that the traders agreed that the probability of a terrorist attack was 4% at the end of 2009. As seen in Figure 2.1, this price has changed a lot during the last seven years. This is due to the fact that traders kept receiving new information during this period, which led them to adapt their beliefs about this issue. In the case of new information arising concerning the probability of an attack against the USA before the end of 2011, traders would buy shares at the current price, which in turn will raise the price on the market.

This security is a winner-takes-all contract used to predict the outcome of binary events. As stated, it pays off only if the underlying event occurs and the price represents its occurring probability. Markets of this type have applications to decision-making, and have proved to be an accurate predictor of future events.

2.2. Definitions

There are many definitions and terminologies for prediction markets. The most common are Idea Futures markets (IF), prediction markets, information markets, virtual stock markets (VSM), securities trading of concepts markets (STOC), decision markets and collective forecasting market. Hanson, one of the inventors of this concept wrote:

> "Information markets can be used to elicit a collective estimate of the expected value or probability of a random variable, reflecting information dispersed across an entire population of traders. The market prediction is not usually an average or median of individual opinions, but is a complex summarization reflecting the game-theoretic interplay of traders as they obtain and leverage information, and as they react to the actions of others obtaining and leveraging their own information." [82]

In his attempt to legalize prediction markets used for research purposes, Bell [8] proposed some definitions to characterize scientific prediction exchanges (SPEx):

1. A *scientific prediction exchange* is a forum that uses instrumentalities of interstate commerce to facilitate the buying and selling of prediction certificates.
2. A *prediction certificate* is a document promising to pay its bearer a specified amount of money on condition that a designated prediction judge names as true the document's prediction claim or claims.
3. A *prediction claim* is an answer to an unresolved question of science, technology, or public policy that can be resolved primarily by the application of skill. A prediction claim is not an answer to an unresolved question about the outcome of a sporting event or contest, or the future value of a securities transaction currently regulated by the Securities Exchange Commission.

Currently, researchers from different disciplines study prediction markets: politics, economy, law, finance, decision science and computer science.

This leads to various research topics and applications. Moreover, each of them tends to use different terminologies to name these markets. In Table 2.1, we summarize the most used concepts and show their particularities.

Table 2.1.: Various implementations of the market concept

Concepts	Outcome	Implementations
Prediction market	Real and testable propositions	SPEx, NewsFuture
Information market	Knowledge aggregation	VSM
Preference market	Simple preference	STOC
Idea market	Idea generation	Imagination Market
Decision market	Policies	N/A

In the following sections, we will review the prediction market literature under four main categories: (1) general description and open problems, (2) theoretical works, (3) applications and (4) law and policy. These main categories are taken from the classification framework based on the nature of prediction markets research used by Tziralis and Tatsiopoulos [165] in their literature review.

2.3. General description

Prediction markets, given their origin, are powerful tools for decision making. They provide incentives for both revelation and discovery of information and provide an algorithm to aggregate this information [171]. Given these incentives, they also support our collective ability to share information [74]. They help the evolution of ideas, "creating a visible consensus of relevant experts, and better incentives for honesty and care when making contributions" [72]. Moreover, they provide this aggregated information in the form of an easily understandable indicator, the price of the shares.

Researches and experiments shows that the main benefits of prediction markets are: efficiency, freedom, flexibility and motivation [109]. They help to make contributors aware of the topic's underlying issues and motivate them to rapidly share their beliefs with the rest of the players. In an organization, these markets encourage collaborators to position themselves regarding the outcome of the company's relevant issues and support the company in becoming more transparent in the way they assess these issues. Leveraging the knowledge of the whole organization, prediction markets are drivers to initiate explanations and to increase comprehension within the company [141].

Empirical evidence and economic theories suggest that prediction markets' predictions "equal or outperform predictions made by groups, voting, experts, and opinion averaging" [44]. Often used to assess corporate or political issues, deliberating groups frequently fail to make good predictions. They are subject to various biases, the most important being social pressures and group dynamics, leading to incomplete information disclosure. "As a result, deliberation often produces a series of unfortunate results: the amplification of errors, hidden profiles, cascade effects, and group polarization" [160]. Prediction markets tend to reduce these errors, providing economic rewards for completely disclosing information and for correcting others' predictions [161]. Their aggregation mechanism reduces individual errors instead of amplifying them as happens in group deliberation. This often leads to better and more informed decisions.

Spann and Skiera [156] evaluate the potential use and different design possibilities as well as the forecast accuracy and performance of prediction markets compared to expert prediction for their application to business forecasting. Furthermore, they propose a new validity test for prediction markets' forecasts.

Graefe and Weinhardt [58] and Berg et al. [14] found that prediction markets are also good predictors for long-term problems. Comparing prediction markets with the Delphi method Graefe and Weinhardt [58] conclude that both offer similar results for long-term forecasts. Moreover, due to the underlying trading mechanism, prediction markets are able to provide an "implicit mechanism for measuring participants' confidence as well as weighting their judgments" [58]. Berg et al. [14] found that "prediction markets prove accurate at long and short forecasting horizons, in absolute terms and relative to natural alternative forecasts". In addition, they are thriftier in terms of resource consumption compared to Delphi studies.

2.4. Information gathering

Traders on a prediction market, as well as on other markets like stock exchanges, are motivated by their potential trading profits. Prediction markets derive two benefits from this motivation: it attracts traders to be active on the market, sharing information and beliefs, and it helps in gathering information. In an equilibrium state, the only way to improve one's profit is to add new information into the market. This results in a great incentive to discover more information and share it in the market [173]. Moreover, because of the opportunity for realizing bigger profits by being the first to discover new information, prediction markets are very fast in aggregating new information. Slamka et al. [151] found in experiments that new information was incorporated in less than 90 seconds on average. They also found that the predictive accuracy increased as consequence of this new information. Wolfers and Zitzewitz [174] also found that market prices rapidly respond to new information and thus that few arbitrage opportunities exist.

Researches on prediction markets [68, 100] show that "the most informed answer will come from an efficient market" [44]. Berg et al. [14] studied the efficiency of prediction markets and concluded that the time series of prices is "consistent with efficient random walks". Rhode and Strumpf [138] reached the same conclusion studying a century of presidential betting markets. To achieve this efficiency, prediction markets should remain liquid, allowing traders to continuously update probabilities. Kambil [88] suggests three criteria to guarantee this liquidity: enough traders, enough knowledgeable participants and enough incentive to trade. Comparing prediction markets and financial markets, Tetlock [162] concludes that the former stay efficient despite low liquidity and volume. Christiansen [33] studied the efficiency of small markets and found that markets above a minimum threshold of 16 participants remain efficient. However, we currently lack real world studies to determine a threshold function based on the forecasting goal of the market. This could lead to less efficient markets and result in poor predictions.

2.5. Information aggregation

The main function of prediction markets is to gather and aggregate dispersed information and publish it for all to see [132]. This aggregating mechanism is based on an efficient market hypothesis. At the equilibrium price, all available information is aggregated in the price [46]. It is then accepted that the equilibrium price corresponds to the traders' mean belief regarding the outcome. Manski [112] found that there could be a substantial difference between the traders' mean belief that the outcome will occur and its equilibrium price when traded as a binary contract. He based his demonstration on the fact that traders are willing to risk a fixed amount. Gjerstad [57] responded, showing that both the risk aversion and the distribution of traders' beliefs affect the equilibrium price. He stated that "for coefficients of relative risk aversion near those estimated in empirical studies and for plausible belief distributions, the equilibrium price is very near the traders' mean belief". Wolfers and Zitzewitz [172] and Snowberg et al. [153] came to the same conclusions. However, they also found that the "efficacy of the forecasts may be undermined somewhat for prices close to $0 or $1, when the distribution of beliefs is either especially disperse, or when trading volumes are somehow constrained, or motivated by an unusual degree of risk-acceptance".

Servan-Schreiber [145] proposes that "the key driver of accuracy seems to be the betting proposition itself: on the one hand, a wager attracts contrarians, which enhances the diversity of opinions that are aggregated. On the other hand, the mere prospect of reward or loss promotes more objective, less passionate thinking, thereby enhancing the opinions that are aggregated". Berg et al. [14] in their study of the Iowa Electronic Market

(IEM) conclude that the market outperformed traditional forecasting methods and that the predictions were very accurate. Chen et al. [30] did some experiments on the equilibrium of prediction markets and suggest that (1) prediction markets are guaranteed to converge to an equilibrium, representing a consensus among the traders; (2) they converge to the equilibrium in at most n rounds of trading, where n is the number of traders; (3) the best possible prediction it can make is the direct communication equilibrium, at which price it equals the expectation of the value of the function based on the information of all traders; but (4) a prediction market is not guaranteed to converge to this best possible prediction.

Wu et al. [176] studied the overconfidence and found that "overconfidence is a widespread phenomenon which is influenced by a number of factors, such as, the difficulty of the judgment task, the amount and nature of outcome feedback, and the gender and culture of the trader". Nevertheless, given that the overconfidence is not equally spread among traders, this will result in potential trading profits for the less overconfident ones. On the same topic, Wolfers and Zitzewitz [172] shows that it is important for prediction markets to attract enough uninformed traders. These traders will issue a flow of uninformed orders, inducing trading profit opportunities for more informed traders and resulting in better forecasting.

Finally, Gruca and Berg [63] propose that prediction markets are able to improve upon publicly available information. In the case of biased public information, traders, motivated by their potential trading profits, are encouraged to "de-bias" this information. This will result in more accurate predictions than those generated by the public information.

2.6. Manipulations

Like traditional markets, prediction markets could be subject to foul play or other distortions. We will address the two principal ones: bubbles and manipulations.

Bubbles are mostly the result of biased public information and group dynamics. Frequent in traditional financial markets, they also appear in prediction markets. As the same rules should apply to both types of exchange, we have currently no way to detect these bubbles in prediction markets. Thus, in experimental markets, bubbles often burst and this results in more accurate predictions [171]. Recent political prediction markets were subject to these bubbles.

In prediction markets, manipulations are a lesser concern than in traditional markets. In both cases, manipulations result in profit opportunities. Manipulations will lead manipulators to lose money, increasing the reward for informed traders and thus ultimately improving the price accuracy [78]. Moreover, in most prediction markets, traders receive the same endowment of play money or are constrained by spending caps, limiting their ability to consistently manipulate the market. Rhode and Strumpf [138] studied a century of manipulations in prediction and betting markets and found that attempts at manipulating these markets generally failed. Furthermore, he suggests that it is difficult and expensive to manipulate prediction markets beyond short periods of time. Moreover, Hanson and Opera [82] found "that a manipulator can substitute for a liquidity trader or for trader irrationality to produce an information market equilibrium".

Finally, even if the same distortions and foul play exist as in traditional markets, we have seen that the outcomes of these manipulations mostly favor better prediction accuracy. Moreover, these manipulations are typically reverted in a short time.

2.7. Market mechanisms

The central aspect of the prediction market aggregation mechanism is how buyers and sellers are matched. A match between a buy and a sell order results in the aggregation of new information and in the creation of a new equilibrium price. The most widely used trading mechanism is the continuous double auction (CDA). To improve the liquidity and accuracy of prediction markets, they also often rely on automated market makers. The most used algorithms are the market scoring rules (MSR) and the dynamic pari-mutuel markets (DPM).

The main idea in incorporating a market maker is to allow traders to trade at different times, serving as an intermediary. The market maker substitutes for traders having different trading times. Thus, it allows the first to trade at a given time, making an offer, and then later, making the opposite offer to other traders. It is a way of allowing asynchronous trading on prediction markets. "By adjusting prices in his favor, a market maker can even profit from providing this service" [81]. Moreover, market makers can encourage trading activity. "Losses of a market maker are gains to its traders, and the prospect of such gains should entice more trading". When the number of participants is small, market makers prevent falling in illiquid markets [1]. Pennock [126] summarizes the advantages of market makers "with regard to three desirable properties of trading mechanisms for prediction markets, namely continuous incorporation of information, guaranteed liquidity, and avoidance of financial risk for the market operator".

2.7.1. Continuous Double Auction

The continuous double auction (CDA) is the most used trading mechanism in prediction markets, as it is in financial markets. It allows traders to submit buy or sell orders which are directly executed against opposite orders or stored in an order book. Orders that are queued in the order book are processed iteratively as soon as opposite orders are submitted or they are cancelled as soon as they expire. The main advantage of this mechanism is that it poses no financial risk for the market operator. This is the main reason for their implementation in most real money markets. "Moreover, the CDA allows for continuous information incorporation into prices and consequently traders are capable of quickly reacting to events in case of liquid markets" [108]. However, the CDA could lead to situations where the market became illiquid with few traders as this is often the case with prediction markets, when the bid–ask spread is too broad or when the order book is empty. Thus, to solve this issue, one should consider the implementation of an automatic market maker.

2.7.2. Market Scoring Rules

Hanson is the father of the market scoring rules (MSR) and its variations. "In practice, scoring rules elicit good probability estimates from individuals, while betting markets elicit good consensus estimates from groups. Market scoring rules combine these features, eliciting estimates from individuals or groups, with groups costing no more than individuals" [80]. Thus, the MSR provides infinite liquidity to the market given a defined range. MSR could be seen as "sequentially used proper scoring rules maintaining a probability distribution over all events" [108]. Traders can improve the prediction, changing the probability by moving the price to a new prediction. New information is immediately incorporated as the probability change. Berg and Proebsting [12] derived all necessary formulae to implement an MSR.

Abramowicz [1] describes a quadratic market scoring rule which is an adaptation of Hanson's MSR. "Its prime virtue is that it provides uniform liquidity across the probability or prediction spectrum. Market participants will thus have the same incentive to do research that is expected to produce an expected change in the market prediction, regardless of the current prediction".

2.7.3. Dynamic Pari-Mutuel

A dynamic pari-mutuel (DPM) acts as hybrid between a pari-mutuel market and a CDA, inheriting some of the advantages of both. "Like a pari-mutuel market, a DPM offers infinite buy-in liquidity and zero risk for the market institution; like a CDA, a DPM can continuously react to new information, dynamically incorporate information into prices, and allow traders to lock in gains or limit losses by selling prior to event resolution" [126]. Offering infinite buy-in liquidity, the DPM "acts as a one-sided market maker always offering to sell at some price and moving the price according to demand" [108]. Traders wanting to sell have to use the order book as the DPM makes no buy offers. The pari-mutuel being redistributive, money goes in a central pool and is redistributed among the winners. Thus, there are no risks for the market operator. Luckner [108] highlights a shortcoming of DPM. Given that there is no incentive to buy early, the best strategy is to wait until the last moment to buy. The first real life implementation of the DPM was the Yahoo! Tech Buzz Game run in 2005 [111].

Finally, we will review two topics related to the trading mechanism: the endowment and the payment scheme.

Seemann et al. [144] did extensive research on the effect of stock endowments on the liquidity of prediction markets. They found that the stock endowments significantly improve the liquidity of the markets. Stock endowments motivate participants to trade stocks that they would never have considered otherwise. Moreover, in order to free liquidity, they have to trade a part of their stock endowment, bringing more information to the market. They also discovered that traders who received stock endowments traded more than twice as many stocks than other participants. In conclusion, they recommend to "provide stock and cash endowment to participants instead of pure cash endowments wherever feasible" [144].

Considering the payment scheme, Luckner [107] showed that performance-based payment schemes do not necessarily lead to better prediction accuracy. He explains this with the risk aversion of traders. Competitive environments like rank-order tournaments should produce the best prediction accuracy. Rank-order tournaments are the most used payment scheme in current prediction markets.

2.8. Applications

There are different uses and case studies of prediction markets. On one side, we have numerous public prediction markets like the Iowa

Electronic Markets (IEM), Foresight Exchange (FX), Hollywood Stock Exchange (HSX), InklingMarkets or NewsFutures. On the other side, there are more and more experiments being made within organizations. Unfortunately, they are poorly investigated and there is a real lack of studies concerning these business applications. However, we found relevant reports on applications by HP, Google, Siemens, BestBuy and GE.

2.8.1. Public prediction markets

Public play-money prediction markets are mostly showcases for prediction markets software vendors. Their main goal is to demonstrate their functionality and their capabilities. We will see later that there is a huge gap between these public marketplaces and their implementation in business contexts. On their side, real-money prediction markets, with the exception of the IEM, are mostly related to gambling platforms.

To attract enough traders or gamblers, public prediction markets have to choose sticky claims and to focus on mass interest topics like sport events, box office, elections or "people"-related news.

Iowa Electronic Market IEM is a well-known real-money prediction market, run by the University of Iowa [16]. Created in 1988, it is the longest-running real-money prediction market. Often cited for its election markets [48], the IEM was also used for many different topics like the Google IPO [17], the incidence of influenza or movie box office receipts [62, 64]. After 20 years of experiments, the IEM is the richest source of studies on prediction markets. Berg et al. [20] summarize the main facts learned from these experiments. First of all, traders are not a random sample of the voting population. This is a very important finding regarding prediction markets [65]. It confirms that the traders must not be representative of the aimed population. This mostly explains their efficiency compared to polls. Next, traders are biased by their preferences. Even if they are asked to predict the outcome of an issue, they tend to act with their own preference in mind. However, the presence of informed traders and their expectation of making a profit efficiently correct this deviation. Further, Gruca and Berg [63] and Berg et al. [13] found that the IEM prices are accurate, both relative to the next best alternative (polls) and in absolute terms. Berg et al. [13] also show that "IEM prices were more stable than polls, responded less to transient events than polls, and were closer to election outcomes than the average poll when the election was more than one week away". Finally, they found that the IEM prices respond quickly to news [127]. Such ability was already well known in traditional stock markets. For example, Maloney and Mulherin [110] found that in 1986, the NYSE correctly identified the guilty company for the crash of Challenger within hours, whereas it took months for the experts to come to the same conclusion.

Hollywood Stock Exchange HSX is a prediction market along the same lines as the IEM, which allows people to use virtual currency to speculate on movie-related questions like box office success and outcomes of the Oscars awards. Pennock et al. [128] found that "prices of movie stocks are good predictors of actual box office performance, and that prices of award securities serve as accurate likelihood assessments of eventual winners". They also observed that traders underpriced the best-performing movies while they overpriced worst-performing ones. This phenomenon, also called the favourite-longshot bias, was heavily studied [18, 42, 94, 152] but no significant effect on the market accuracy was detected. Finally, Pennock et al. [128] compared the results of the HSX market with five experts' opinions and found that the market's score surpassed the scores of all five experts individually, and of their consensus.

TradeSports and Intrade Both these real-money public prediction markets or gambling forums were run by the same company but are now separated. Created initially for sports events, they now hosts a rich set of political, financial, entertainment and sports contracts. Borghesi [23] studied the 2002, 2003 and 2004 NFL seasons on TradeSports and found that "asset values differ significantly from prices only between kickoff and contract expiry". Moreover, he discovered that the contracts are subject to being overpriced after new information arrive—in this case, a goal—especially when the incoming news is negative. Tetlock [162] observed that "there is a significant reverse favorite-longshot bias in contracts based on sports games on TradeSports; but there is no such bias in financial contracts". This is surprising, considering that both the players and the market mechanism were the same. So in conclusion, he found that financial markets for short-term contracts are relatively efficient despite numerous obstacles to arbitrage.

Finally, TradeSports was subject to two studies on the incidence of real-money versus play-money on the market accuracy. Servan-Schreiber et al. [146] and Rosenbloom and Notz [140] compared the results of both TradeSports and NewsFuture. The first ones compared the 2003/04 NFL season on both markets. They found, as expected, that the prediction markets were both more accurate than individual humans. Furthermore, they found that the play-money market performed as well as the real-money market. They tried to explain this similarity by the presence of "two opposing forces: real-money markets may better motivate information discovery while play-money markets may yield more efficient information aggregation. Rosenbloom and Notz [140], in their study, used a sequential probability ratio test (SPRT) to compare the results of NFL, DJIA and US team sports (basketball and baseball) markets. Like Servan-Schreiber et al. [146], they found no statistical differences between the real-money and play-money NFL markets. However, the DJIA market showed that TradeSports was clearly superior to the play-money News-Futures. Unfortunately there are currently no theoretical explanations to understand this difference. Thus, if these results could be replicated, it could severely trouble the adoption of prediction markets for business applications given the legal and technical hurdles linked to the use of real-money platforms.

Foresight Exchange FX is a play-money prediction market to test the ability to predict the outcome of future events, check the odds of upcoming events, and make bets on, among other things, science and technology events. It was launched in 1994 as a testbed for Hanson's Idea Future market. Although it has been running for a long time now, there are almost no studies concerning its design or mechanism. Five years after the launch of FX, Kittlitz [91] published his experiences and raised some issues. The first one refers to the claim wording. As FX was the first market offering traders the possibility of creating their own claims, they encountered various problems concerning claim wording and judgment. To overcome these issues, they implemented a dedicated mailing-list to discuss the wording of claims before their release on the market. Furthermore, as FX assesses mostly long-term issues, Pennock et al. [129] found that its forecasts "strongly correlate with outcome frequencies". Thus, it is not yet known if prediction markets are able to provide reliable forecasts of events which will only be settled in 10 or more years.

Tech Buzz Game Yahoo! Research launched its play-money market in collaboration with O'Reilly concerning the future of technology. It is also the first market using the dynamic pari-mutuel (DPM) automated market maker algorithm from Pennock [126]. Each share on the platform was associated with a *buzz score*–the number of search for a certain word during the past seven days on yahoo.com. Traders were invited to trade according to both the stock price and the buzz score, buying stocks where prices appear low compared to expected future buzz scores [111]. Chen et al. [31] studied more carefully the predictability of DPMs. They examined whether prices of stocks follow their underlying values and also "whether buzz scores increase (decrease) over time in the future when the market implied buzz scores are higher (lower) than the current actual buzz scores". Both methods confirmed that the DPM succeeds in forecasting event trends. Moreover, they compared human traders with robots placing random orders. Evidences show that, on average, traders made a profit whereas robots made loss, confirming the predictability of DPMs.

Policy Analysis Market A final example of public prediction markets is the controversial and rapidly aborted PAM, or FutureMap [79, 77, 137, 134] sponsored by the US Department of Defense, which was intending to allow speculating about strategic and geopolitical issues. The cancellation of the project was more a reaction against its supervisor, John Poindexter, and the Bush administration who named it to this function than against the project itself. Thus, the resignation of Poindexter ensured the end of the project.

The goal of the project was to test the ability of prediction markets to forecast overall geopolitical trends. Using a new combinatorial trading technology (MSR) it should have been able to estimate the effects of various policies, for example, betting "on the chance of high levels of civil unrest in Saudi Arabia in the fourth quarter of 2004, conditional on the US moving its troops out of there two quarters earlier" [79].

After the cancellation, Hanson, the main researcher working on this project, presented five design issues related to *real terrorism futures* [79], as this was the main argument used by the senators against the policy analysis market: (1) combinatorics, (2) manipulation, (3) moral hazard, (4) hiding prices and (5) decision selection bias. He also shows that these problems are not insurmountable and that *real terrorism futures* appears to be technically realistic. In March 2007, Weigle, a colonel at the US Army War College, wrote a proposal to use prediction markets as another tool in the intelligence kitbag [170]. He concludes that prediction markets "will not reveal brilliant insights about terrorist intentions; they won't provide tactical initiative but may prevent strategic surprise".

2.8.2. Enterprise prediction markets

There are currently many companies running experiments on prediction markets to support business forecasts. These forecasts are very broad: sales, new products, project management, etc. Thus, there is currently not much published research on these internal markets. We will therefore focus on some published experiments made by Siemens, Google, HP, GE and Rite Solutions, which present interesting results and are an important source of inspiration for our own design. Most results were related to the behavior of the markets in the business environment rather than to modeling issues, giving us more insight on real-life setups.

Siemens In 1997, the University of Technology Vienna ran a six-month prediction market experiment at Siemens Austria to support decisions in project management [123, 122]. Given that project management techniques often fail to rapidly recognize delays and problems, generally due to a unwillingness to inform about these issues, Siemens was looking for a tool to better collect this information from knowledgeable people. In fact, people involved in these problems could be afraid of suffering negative feedback when communicating about them. So, in order to improve their project management process, Siemens decided to use prediction markets as a tool to anonymously aggregate and evaluate information on project issues. They ran an internal prediction market to predict the progress (due date) of a software project to improve their conventional planning tools.

Two hundred engineers were asked to invest real money in the market to predict the finishing date as exactly as possible. Sixty people invested 100 ATS of their own money in addition to 200 ATS provided as an endowment by the company after a brief introductory meeting. The question asked was: "Can the project be finished in the planned time horizon". Traders could choose to invest in a winner-takes-all contract or a contract with a linear payoff function based on the delay (sooner or later) in weeks. Ortner [122] found that after a month, the price on the two markets was quite stable. Moreover, at the end of the experiment, "25% of the traders mentioned that they had problems with the use of the market". He suggests that traders need some time to become familiar with the tool (concepts) and the software (user interface) before producing relevant aggregated information. He also noticed that in order to be more productive, participants need an extensive training before opening the market.

The results of the market were impressive as they correctly predicted a delay of 2–3 weeks (13 days in practice) 3 month before the scheduled deadline. Participants "anticipated new information, rumors and personal feelings long before official sources published official statements". Based on this success, Siemens ran a second experiment "to predict shifts in estimated expenditures of large software projects".

Google From 2005 to 2007, Google launched the largest corporate prediction market experiments. The market was used to forecast product launch dates, new office openings and many other items of strategic importance to Google. Each quarter, they created about 25–30 different markets based on winner-takes-all claims. The payoff was a lottery incentive based on traders' performance.

Cowgill et al. [37] show that the market suffered some biases, remaining reasonably efficient. These biases were mostly due to employee optimism and favorite bias. Studying these biases, Cowgill et al. [37] found that they were "partly driven by the trading of newly hired employees", more experienced employees being better calibrated. This finding suggests that "corporate prediction markets may perform better as collective experience increases". This seems to go against recent experiments lasting couple of minutes or hours.

Moreover, Cowgill et al. [37] found that the prediction market was able to provide insight into how organizations process information. They observed the physical location in the buildings of employees placing orders. They also followed the frequent office moves of the traders. They concluded that there is a strong correlation between the opinions expressed on the market and the physical proximity of employees.

HP Plott and Chen [133] present the deployment of a real-money information aggregation mechanism (IAM) inside Hewlett-Packard for the purpose of making printer sales forecasts, showing that IAM performed better than traditional methods employed inside Hewlett-Packard. Between 7 and 24 traders from marketing and finance departments as well from HP Labs were active on 12 one-week markets during the three years of the experiment. Traders from HP Labs where included in the experiment to increase the liquidity of the market, although they had no real information to share on the market. There were important participation variations between the markets with a tendency to lose participants over time, ending with seven active participants for the final experiment. Moreover, the markets were only open during lunch and after work time.

Despite there being a very low participation, Plott and Chen [133] show that (1) IAM predictions outperformed official HP forecasts, (2) market probability distributions are consistent with actual outcomes and (3) "IAM makes accurate qualitative predictions about the direction that the actual outcome will occur (above or below) relative to the official forecast". Furthermore, this experiment shows that prediction markets could be efficiently used in a corporate environment. The main advantages of prediction markets in this context are their flexibility (they can aggregate any type of information spread throughout an organization), their scalability (they can support any number of participants, geographical repartition or duration) and their incentive to reveal the truth. However, in spite of these results, the main unresolved issue encountered during these experiments was the lack of participation and the difficulty of motivating them to be active on the market, as shown in other real-world experiments.

GE In order to elicit and rank-order ideas on new technologies, products and research areas, GE designed the Imagination Market and used it more than ten times in various contexts and for different purposes [96, 157]. The Imagination Market is a "preference market" designed to support the ideation process for large and globally distributed teams, allowing continuous contributions and ranking of ideas [96]. They chose to use such markets to overcome the principal issues they encountered with traditional methods like brainstorming sessions or suggestion boxes and studied the effectiveness of information markets "as an idea generation and ranking tool" [96].

LaComb et al. [97] made a very in-depth study of designing information markets, discussing various common issues like payoff functions, incentive mechanisms and market mechanisms. She proposes a comprehensive list of information market design factors to help building such tools. Nevertheless, given the variety of applications potentially based on information markets, this list is more a specifically targeted subset for the Imagination Market.

Two different experiments ran at GE [96, 157] conclude that information markets are quite good at supporting ideation processes, but don't overcome traditional methods for ranking elicited ideas. The additional benefits resulting from this approach include "providing immediate feedback, allowing visibility of all ideas to all contributors, and being a fun mechanism for consensus building". In conclusion, GE's experiments show that information markets are more efficient in generating and eliciting ideas than traditional methods, resulting in more valuable ideas for the enterprise. However, they are not better in ranking these ideas, given the results of the experiments. To be sure that this is really the case, one would have to do further research in this area, using both approaches (traditional and information market) on the same sample.

Rite-Solutions The Innovation Engine is an information market based on the same principles as the Imagination Market from GE. The goal of the Innovation Engine is to "develop a mechanism that could *operationalize* innovation by tapping the collective genius in the organization in a non-intimidating, fun way to generate these good ideas continuously" [98]. The engine works with the whole ideation process in the company, supporting each step of the process. Employees can draft a new idea, find a broker to help them to refine their idea and make the IPO. Once announced, the idea can be bought by other employees and added to their portfolio, raising the price of this idea. The 20 most valued ideas are budgeted to get official support from the company. After that, they enter a phase where all employees can work on these ideas given their own competencies and preferences for supporting the realization of the inventors' ideas. If successful, the idea is removed from the market and the inventor and investors are rewarded based on a reward plan elaborated at the same time as the budget.

As Lavoie [98] is the CEO of the company, the findings from this case are based on his own experiences with the engine in solving innovation process issues. First, it allows every employee to be part of the process, not only the leaders or the most extrovert. This allows the majority of the *intellectual bandwidth* to drive the company. It also supports 24/7 innovation, compared to "just-in-time" innovation as implied by traditional methods. Finally, it provokes thought. Employees are motivated to participate in the process, buying shares of good ideas or helping inventors to take their idea further. So far the results using the Innovation Engine at Rite-Solutions are very encouraging and have generated many successful ideas resulting in new products or patents.

The Rite-Solutions study confirms the results obtained at GE, stating that information markets are very efficient in supporting an ideation process. Furthermore, given the relative lack of success in ranking ideas at GE, the Innovation Engine approach should be considered for further developments. Not only using financial valuation, but also valuing the willingness to actively support the idea working on it, this approach seems to be better at catching the real value of the ideas. This approach goes one step further in crowd-sourcing the ideation process.

2.8.3. Experiments with business prediction markets

STOC The MIT Securities Trading of Concepts or STOC used the pricing mechanism for marketing research using a pseudo-securities market to measure preferences relating to new products. Participants were asked to "express their preferences over new product concepts by trading virtual securities" [27]. This application differs from traditional prediction markets in that there is no external objective "truth" that can be used to settle the market. It must be put in the family of the preference markets. In three experiments, between 20 and 60 participants were asked to give their preferences on bicycle pumps, crossover vehicles and laptop bags. Each experiment was empirically tested against preferences measured through traditional methods. The "experiments reveal that the market prices of securities designed to represent product concepts are remarkably efficient, accurate, and internally consistent measures of preferences, even when conducted with relatively few traders" [27].

The goal of STOC is to assess preferences for product concepts that may never come into existence and may never have actual outcomes, like assessing R&D portfolios. Traders were given 10–60 minutes to give their preferences, buying or selling product concepts. Unlike prediction markets, the only information available was the product information, the trader's personal preferences, their expectation of others' preferences and the price movements. The only incentive was peer recognition. Using a volume-weighted average price (VWAP) they tried to predict potential market share for various product prototypes. Results are encouraging, as the STOC performed better than traditional methods in the majority of the cases. Chan et al. [27] also "note the importance of clear and salient stimuli, and the need for training and priming traders prior to the start of STOC games". Lack of good stimuli led to bad results, as did the lack of good claim description in traditional prediction markets.

New Product Development "Preference markets address the need for scalable, fast and engaging market research in new product development (NPD)" [38]. Currently, with the emergence of crowd-sourcing, companies are confronted with new issues related to NPD. To address customers' needs and propositions, they need to prioritize hundreds of design decisions. To support this process, preference markets offers a flexible prioritization methodology for product features and concepts. The benefits of these markets include "speed (less than one hour per trading experiment), scalability (question capacity grows linearly with the number of traders) and flexibility (features and concepts can be tested simultaneously)" [38].

To address these issues, Dahan et al. [38] designed a preference market based on a double-auction mechanism with a random end to avoid boundary effects at the end of trading. Stocks were representing various mutually exclusive product choices. The scalability was assured by randomly assigning small groups of traders to small groups of stocks, where the same stocks were traded by more than one group, to allow for cross-testing between the trader groups. They found that "preference markets can be scalable by virtue of an experimental design that matches traders with a convenient number of stocks, and creating trading links between the groups" [38]. They also validated the idea that self preferences influence expectations of others more than others influence self preferences. Moreover, Soukhoroukova and Spann [155] show that preference markets for NPD are very efficient in terms of required participants compared to traditional methods requiring more than ten times as many participants. Furthermore, it is relatively easy to find participants for preference market experiments, compared with traditional market research methods.

2.9. Law and policy

2.9.1. Legality and regulation

Since 1988 and the launch of the IEM, the legality of prediction markets is a recurring topic among scientists. In February 1992, the IEM received a no-action letter from the CFTC concerning the 2002 presidential election market that allowed them to run academic prediction market experiments with small investments ($500). [1] Thus, this no-action letter concerns only the IEM and does not preclude having to comply with state laws.

Currently, there are two main legal issues concerning prediction markets in the USA: compliance with the CFTC and with the gambling regulations. Concerning the CFTC, even if the "means and ends of prediction materially differ from the means and ends of commodity futures markets" [9] they would probably be subject the CFTC regulation. Bell [9] argues that the "laws that menace prediction markets do so almost accidentally. Those statutes and regulations arose in response to quite different transactions, long before anyone had even conceived of prediction markets". Thus, the current uncertainty holds back operators from running such markets,

1. No-action letter from Andrea M. Corcoran, Director, Commodity Futures Trading Commission (CFTC) Division of Trading and Markets, to George R. Neumann, Professor of Economics, University of Iowa (5 February 1992); `http://www.cftc.gov/files/foia/repfoia/foirf0503b002.pdf`

which slows down the research [105], and it also discourages people using them, being afraid of committing a crime by so doing.

However, there are some signs that prediction markets could avoid the CFTC regulation. First of all, prediction markets differs from securities markets in that they transfer wealth between informed and less foresighted traders while securities markets merely amass it [9]. Thus, prediction markets could fall under the "hybrid instrument" exclusion from CFTC jurisdiction, "winning their preemptive protection from state gaming and bucket shop laws" [9]. Moreover, being subject to CFTC regulations will definitely raise the opportunity cost of running such markets. Many papers discuss strategies to deal with this issue. First of all, companies operating internal prediction markets should ensure that their markets do not support significant hedging functions and treat their market's claims and prices as trade secrets [10]. Furthermore, they should clearly notify the traders that the market does not deal in CFTC regulated instruments.

In the case of a regulation, Hahn [69] proposes that the federal government "implements a clear policy that allows information markets that serve a useful economic purpose" and that the CFTC regulates them. To lower the impact of this regulation on small experiments, they also propose that small-stake prediction markets that limit the size of investments or stay below certain volume or revenue caps should be exempted from the CFTC regulations. Furthermore, in the case of internal prediction markets, firms should be allowed to self-certify their prediction market contracts. However, Bell [9] proposes the creation of a federal *Scientific Prediction Exchange Act* to guarantee that the CFTC would have no authority over scientific prediction exchanges, arguing that CFTC regulations will unavoidably restrain the adoption of these tools.

The second issue concerning gambling regulations should be addressed at both federal and state levels. There are currently two ways of dealing with it. The easiest one is for it to fall under the CFTC regulation. In this case, prediction markets will be protected from state laws. The other one is to demonstrate that prediction markets do not comply with the requirements of the gambling laws. As gambling supposes prize, chance and consideration, prediction markets emphasize skill-based trading rather than chance. Furthermore, reducing the revenues or forbidding traders from investing their own funds will definitely protect them from these laws [10].

However, for Bell [9] the most probable solution is that "prediction markets will win legal status under US law by default, thanks to what people come to accept as an ordinary and beneficial practice rather than what courts, politicians, or regulators proclaim".

Finally, 19 scholars wrote an open letter in Science, asking the CFTC and Congress to free prediction markets of unnecessary government restrictions [5]. They propose three scenarios where the use of prediction markets should be eligible for safe harbor treatments: first, the not-for-profit platforms operated by research institutions for research purposes, like the IEM; second, platforms operated by government agencies like, the PAM project; third, internal markets operated by corporations with no research goals but limited to their employees or contractors. These exchanges should be self-regulated, given that their operators would make reasonable efforts to keep them free from fraud and manipulation. Moreover, the operators of these markets should be able to test various designs, incentives, payoff functions and manipulation schemes to improve their overall design and help the progress of science.

At the same time, the CFTC issued a Request for Public Comment on *Concept Release on the Appropriate Regulatory Treatment of Event Contracts* [2]. This request seems to show a real willingness on the part of the CFTC to consider reasonable options and arguments for regulating prediction markets. Thus, at the moment, the CFTC seems to only consider not-for-profit, IEM-like prediction markets as exempt from its jurisdiction.

2. `http://www.cftc.gov/stellent/groups/public/@lrfederalregister/documents/file/e8-9981a.pdf`

2.9.2. Public policy and decision making

Many scholars are studying the implications of using prediction markets for public policy. For Ledyard [100] policy analysis is about the acquisition and organization of dispersed information in order to better inform a decision that has to be made. In the context of political decisions, prediction markets "could lead to large potential gains for both individuals, firms, decision makers and the society" [21]. As individuals and firms could better assess their risks based on the probability of various outcomes, decision makers could measure the perceived impact of their decisions, and the society at large would benefit from more informed decisions [76]. For example, Wolfers and Zitzewitz [175] studied the impact of an increase in the probability of war in Iraq on the oil price. They found that a 10% increase in the probability of war was accompanied by a $1 increase in spot oil prices [175].

We will now consider two applications of prediction markets related to public policy. The first one is designed to inform about the consequences of the decisions (advised policy) [21, 44, 76, 100, 175] and the second is designed to inform about the costs and benefits of different projects (performance-based policy) [67, 70].

Advised policy The role of the prediction market is to estimate the consequences of decisions. To achieve this goal, policymakers should create markets offering conditional shares related to the consequences of the policy if it is enforced or not. For example, in the case of the US health insurance, such a market could offer shares based on the estimate of US lifespan in 2020 given that president Obama was able to enforce his project, while other shares will estimate the lifespan given that his project was not enforced. The difference between the two predictions will give the aggregated estimate of the impact of Obama's project on the US lifespan, giving an indicator of the effectiveness of his reform.

To apply prediction markets to policy situations, one should consider two aspects [100]. The first one is that such markets would deal with many correlated contracts. Traditional market mechanisms are not able to support this. Ledyard [100] proposes using Hanson market-scoring rule function supporting conditional contracts [80]. The second is to leverage enough incentive to achieve accurate aggregation of information.

Einbinder [44] distinguishes three types of decisions that should benefit from the use of prediction markets. The first, contingency decisions, are incidental to the prediction and have no impact on the decision itself. For example, a citizen would sell land if the prediction that a motorway will be built nearby rose, but selling land would not impact the prediction itself. The second type of decision affects the prediction but not the definition of the underlying claim. For example, a low prediction for a vote concerning a new museum could motivate politicians to invest more resources in the campaign and hopefully affect the prediction, but the change in the prediction itself will not affect the vote. The last type of decision affects both the prediction and the definition of the underlying claim. In this case, decisions are based on the prediction. For example, one should only enforce a policy if the prediction is greater than a certain percentage. A bad prediction would impact the policy but also the prediction itself, because the cancellation of the policy will also cancel the underlying claim.

Hanson [76] presents seven design issues when dealing with policy markets. These issues concern: the importance of enough of the claims to attract traders; their strong influence to limit the noise; the clear enough settlement rules to avoid ambiguities; the presence of measured outcomes to identify how they were influenced by the decision; the participation of enough informed traders; the creation of enough incentive to disclose all information; the guarantee of the anonymity of the traders; and the difficulty of changing the reality to modify the prediction. In conclusion, policy markets "will not function effectively without the ability to create distinct options that have a measurable influence on relevant aggregate outcomes, and the problem has to be important enough to be worth paying to give traders, some of them insiders, enough incentive to trade" [76].

Performance-based policy This approach combines the use of prediction markets with payments for performance. Hahn and Tetlock [70] present "a framework for designing contracts that provides information on the costs, benefits, and net benefits of different policy proposals". The underlying idea is that the policymaker specifies a performance measure for project benefits and lets it be estimated by a prediction market. The prediction market will estimate the performance measure with and without project realization (this is like our previous example on US health insurance). The difference between the two estimations is the benefit of the project. Then the government, based on the expected benefit will decide to auction the right to implement the project. The resulting auction price is the net benefit. At the end, if the net benefit from auction is greater than the minimum acceptable price, government decides to fund. This process allows government to rely on a more informed assessment of policy proposals. Moreover, carefully analyzing the benefits of each policy will enable a greater availability of assets for financing priority projects.

Hahn and Tetlock [67] show the benefits of using such a method. The contracts could be based on numerous contingencies and could address most of the policies; these markets could efficiently assess critical public policy issues; they provide a strong foundation for implementing a variety of government oversight mechanisms; and they could provide more transparency in governmental decision making.

In conclusion, "combining information markets with paying for performance has the potential to improve how policies are delivered. In addition to providing economic benefits, the system will enable lawmakers to hold bureaucrats more accountable for results. And ultimately, voters will be able to hold their elected officials more accountable for expenditures on economic development" [70]. This new process could substantially change the nature of legislative and regulatory oversight.

2.10. Open problems

Based on the previous literature review and on our interests, we can draw out three problems currently not addressed by the research community and that we will address in this book: (1) key design factors for prediction markets based on the instantiation context, (2) appropriateness of prediction markets for complex predictions (R&D, technology foresight, ideation, ...) and (3) efficiency of prediction markets compared to traditional forecasting methods. There are of course more problems to be addressed in the areas of aggregation mechanisms, legality, efficiency versus adequacy or market maker algorithms, but they are outside the scope of this research.

2.10.1. Key design factors for prediction markets based on the instantiation context

Currently, there are several studies presenting some design factors for prediction markets applied to some specific context. Therefore, it is currently not possible to rely on these factors for building a prediction market platform for a specific usage. We propose to develop a set of necessary design factors to support the design of specific prediction markets based on their implementation context. Our goal is to support the requirement engineering process by providing all the design factors and their values for generic or specific prediction market designs. In Part II, we will collect, define and instantiate these design factors for various prediction market applications.

Practitioners need an exhaustive typology of design factors to support the development and the instantiation of prediction markets in companies.

2.10.2. Appropriateness of prediction markets for complex predictions

Our previous literature survey shows various usages of prediction markets, mostly for elections (which must be distinguished from policies, which are complex issues), sports and entertainment issues. The common denominator of these applications is the relative simplicity of the issues addressed. They can be mostly summarized by "will the event X occurs at time t", where X can be the result of an election, a given number of entries at the box office, a score during a game, even an event conditional to an other one.

We propose to explore new instantiations of prediction markets to solve complex R&D or technological issues. Given their ability to aggregate bits of dispersed information among various stakeholders, prediction markets should be able to help solving complex forecasting issues. Our goal is to design and evaluate new prediction markets to solve forecasting issues in the field of R&D portfolio management and technological foresight. In Part III, we will present three innovative designs and usages of prediction markets.

Research should demonstrate that prediction markets are appropriate and accurate when applied to complex issues like technology assessment.

2.10.3. Efficiency of prediction markets compared to traditional forecasting methods

Finally, even if prediction markets seems to be able to accurately predict the outcome of various issues, their adoption will largely depend on their efficiency compared to established methods, techniques and tools. Various studies showed that the adoption of new technologies or products depends on their internal and external qualities, but also on the effort needed to switch from the old one to the new one. In our context, this effort will be concerned with implementing a new method, using a new tool, learning a new technique, etc. To be successfully diffused and adopted, the benefit of using prediction markets should overcome the effort needed to use them.

Given that there is little room to dramatically improve the accuracy of predictions to overcome the effort needed for their adoption, we propose to show that prediction markets could be more efficient than traditional approaches in specific contexts. Our goal is to show that for specific activities like technological forecasting, prediction markets are more efficient than traditional methods and lead to comparable results. In chapter 7, we will compare two technological forecasting methods and examine their key success factors.

Research should demonstrate that prediction markets are efficient compared to traditional approaches for addressing the assessment of technologies.

Part II.

Design Process

3. Design Science Research

This chapter introduces design science as a type of theory in information systems (IS). We then present design science research (DSR) theory building, methodology and evaluation processes. Finally, we introduce our own research process and the resulting contents of this book.

3.1. Introduction

The nature of the problems we intend to solve in this book naturally leads us to consider using a design science (DS) approach.

According to Weber [169], design science offers IS a much needed paradigm, carving out a niche for that research discipline. Moreover, according to March and Smith [113], there are two legitimate kinds of scientific interest in the information systems domain: (1) a natural and social sciences approach seeking to understand reality, (2) a design science approach aiming at creating artifacts that serve human purposes. The second one is also named "science of the artificial" by Simon [148] and defined as "a body of knowledge about artificial (man-made) objects and phenomena designed to meet certain desired goals". Moreover "rather than being in conflict, however, both activities can be encompassed under a broad notion of science that includes two distinct species termed natural and design science" [113].

Information Systems Design Research (ISDR) emerged in the 1980s and became a distinct line of research in IS in the late 1990s. Even though ISDR has gained in importance during the past 20 years, there is still no widely accepted definition. For Vaishnavi and Kuechler [166], "design research involves the analysis of the use and performance of designed artifacts to understand, explain and very frequently to improve on the behavior of aspects of Information Systems". These artifacts could be IS, but could also take the form of algorithms, human/computer interfaces and system design methodologies or languages. Thus ISDR should not be limited to artifacts, but should also explore "design environments, design education, cognitive processes of design as relevant to the support of the design process and much more topics" [95]. They conclude: "if the core of information systems is the artifact then surely its heart is increasing understanding of every aspect of the design process by which these artifacts are brought into being".

3.2. Understanding DSR

In their widely read paper, Hevner et al. [84] "describe the performance of design-science research in IS via a concise conceptual framework and clear guidelines for understanding, executing, and evaluating the research". The conceptual framework, illustrated in Figure 3.1, consists mainly of three distinctive loops: (1) the relevance loop (addressing a class of problems [167]), (2) the rigor loop (building from and contributing to the knowledge base) and (3) the develop/build and justify/evaluate loop. In this framework, the relevance and rigor loops support and entertain the design activity represented by the develop/build and justify/evaluate loop. During the design process, this loop will be iteratively run, assessing and refining the design, to meet the desired goals.

To support researchers, Hevner et al. [84] developed seven guidelines for "understanding, executing, and evaluating the research". By definition, design science research must produce a viable artifact (Guideline 1) to address important and relevant problems (Guideline 2). This artifact must yield utility, and its quality and efficacy must be rigorously evaluated (Guideline 3). Furthermore, design science research must provide innovative contributions in both areas (Guideline 4) and use rigorous methods to support the build/evaluate process (Guideline 5). The search process induced by this loop, should lead to an effective solution (Guideline 6). Finally, the findings from the design science research should be able to be communicated to both technical and management audiences (Guideline 7). They also state that these guidelines should be carefully used, given the particular research that one would conduct. They are not a checklist to follow step by step to guarantee a successful design science research.

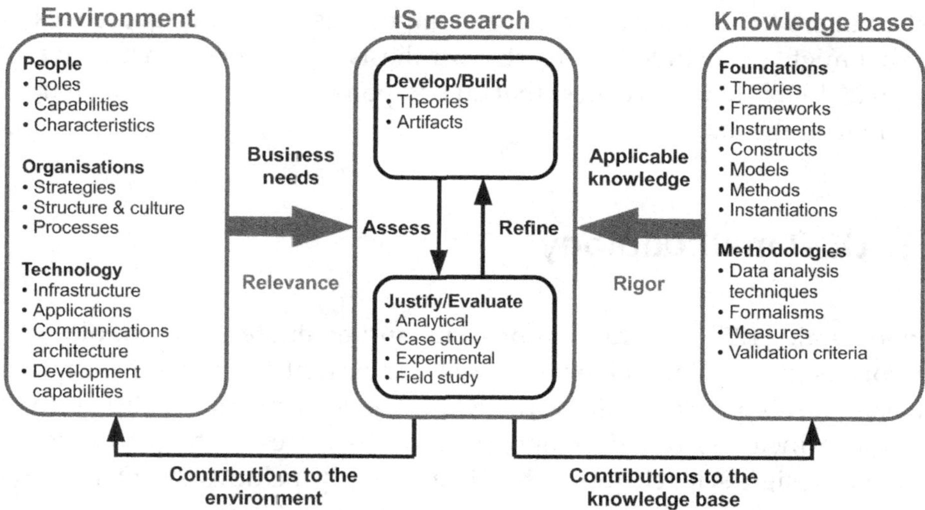

Figure 3.1.: Information systems research framework

3.3. Building a DSR theory

Following Gregor [59] presentation of the five types of theory in IS, and inspired by the work of Walls et al. [167] on the specification of information systems design theories (ISDT), Gregor and Jones [60] developed an anatomy of design theories in IS to address the research conducted using the theory type V (theory for design and action). Their goal is to support "specifying design theory so that it can be communicated, justified, and developed cumulatively" but also to "address explicitly problems associated with the role of instantiations and the specification of design theories for methodologies and interventions as well as for products and applications" [60].

For this purpose, they identified eight components of design theories: (1) purpose and scope, (2) constructs, (3) principles of form and function, (4) artifact mutability, (5) testable propositions, (6) justificatory knowledge (kernel theories), (7) principles of implementation and (8) an expository instantiation. "The listing of the theory components gives some guidelines to what might be included in an article or thesis that reports constructive research" [60]. They also expect that all components would be present in an achieved theory.

3.4. DSR methodology

Peffers et al. [125] present, demonstrate and evaluate a methodology for conducting design science research in IS, that they call a design science research methodology (DSRM). The aim of the DSRM is to provide principles, practices and procedures to researchers to carry effective design science research. The process includes six steps or stages: (1) problem identification and motivation, (2) definition of the objectives for a solution, (3) design and development, (4) demonstration, (5) evaluation and (6) communication. Even if their goal is to formalize the DSRM, the authors also warn that "researchers should by no means draw any inference that the DSRM is the only appropriate methodology with which to conduct such research". They stress this point presenting five alternatives to their DSRM that could be used in the design science research context.

3.5. DSR evaluation

Design science artifacts allow many types of evaluations depending on their form. The rich phenomena that emerge from the interaction of people, organizations and technology could be qualitatively assessed to yield an understanding of the phenomena adequate for theory development or problem solving [93]. As field studies enable behavioral science researchers to understand organizational phenomena in context, the process of constructing and exercising innovative IS artifacts enables design science researchers to understand the problem addressed by the artifact and the feasibility of their approach to its solution [117].

Pries-Heje et al. [136] propose a strategic DSR evaluation framework (Table 3.1) which supports researchers in selecting evaluation strategies. The framework expands the traditional ex post perspective embraced by the majority of the researchers. It "encompasses both ex ante and ex post orientations as well as naturalistic settings (e.g., case studies) and artificial settings (e.g., lab experiments) for DSR evaluation" [136].

Table 3.1.: Strategic DSR evaluation framework

	Ex Ante	**Ex Post**
Naturalistic	Design process / design product	Design process / design product
Artificial	Design process / design product	Design process / design product

3.6. Our DSR process

During the research which resulted in this book we followed a DSRM. Inspired by Peffers et al. [125] and Hevner et al. [84] we iteratively built and evaluated various prediction market designs to support our goals. Given Peffers et al. [125], we mainly followed the design, demonstration and evaluation steps iteration loop three times before concluding.

These three iterations were the occasion to build, test and finally refine our design in various contexts. Furthermore, we chose a different evaluation processes for each iteration loop. This book is structured according the six main DSRM steps as summarized in Figure 3.2.

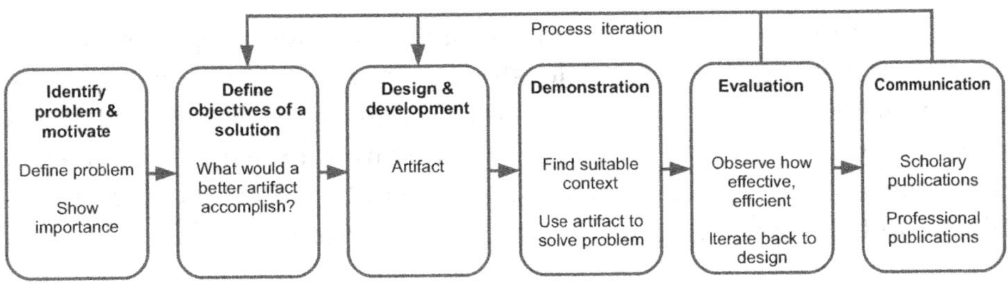

Figure 3.2.: Design science research methodology

Identify problem and motivate In chapter 2, we briefly presented the problems we intend to solve with our new design of prediction markets. We then motivated our choice through an extensive literature review.

Define objectives of a solution In the first sections of chapter 4, we present the design of a prediction market. Starting from the main functions of a marketplace and finishing with a complete typology of prediction market design factors.

Design and development The later sections of chapter 4 present our development process, the main functions of our first prototype and its architecture. In part III, we will further refine and evaluate our artifact in various contexts.

Demonstration and evaluation In part III, we iteratively design, develop, evaluate and refine three artifacts to support various experiments and contexts. The first iteration concludes by presenting five design propositions for prediction markets for technology assessment. The second iteration proposes a new prediction market process to support R&D portfolio management. Finally, we compare the efficiency of prediction markets to traditional approaches like MCDM and propose a comparison framework for technology assessment tools. Each chapter presents a particular usage and context in order to solve one specific problem and finishes with the presentation of our contributions, both academic and professional.

Communication The final part of this work summarizes our findings both for a professional and an academic audience. We also compare our research process with the seven guidelines of Hevner et al. [84], supporting design science research, and outline an information systems design theory based on the eight components of Gregor and Jones [60].

4. Design of a Prediction Market

This chapter determines the main requirements of a prediction market, based on the electronic trading requirements as well as interviews with researchers working for a national competence center in research (NCCR). We then present the main functions and the architecture of such software. Finally, we develop a typology of design factors to support the development of prediction markets and present our own implementation named MarMix.

4.1. Introduction

In 1992, Hanson [72] imagined running prediction markets to help researchers presenting non-mainstream research ideas and getting funded. To achieve this goal, ideas should be published on a marketplace and a fraction of the "value" of these ideas would be given to the researcher to pursue his research.

Our main goal is to build and operate a prediction market to predict the emergence and the evolution of mobile information and communication technologies. This implies developing a modular platform that allows a great flexibility in the definition of the business processes and which also enables us to track all the users' activities and their behaviors on the platform.

To build such a platform, we first identified the general requirements of an electronic trading platform like a stock exchange, conducted interviews with researchers and future users of this platform and, finally, made an extensive literature review to identify the main design factors of a prediction market. Combining these results with our previous literature review in chapter 2 let us define 30 design factors that support the development of a prediction market. Finally, we show how to instantiate these factors to build our first prototype destined to predict the emergence and the evolution of mobile information and communication technologies.

4.2. Electronic trading requirements

To identify the main functions of a prediction market platform, we first choose to rely on the general electronic trading requirements. There are currently many electronic stock exchanges, and their main functions are globally the same. As we have seen, prediction markets are electronic marketplaces for trading securities, and they should support the following functions [158]:

1. Order entry
2. Order execution
3. Order confirmation
4. Transfer of share ownership
5. Making payment
6. Market quotations

A prediction market also acting as a bank and a clearing house holding all the securities and portfolios should also support:

7. Basic account management
8. Account endowment and guarantee
9. Statements of account

4.2.1. Order entry

Traders should be able to submit their orders in an efficient way, choosing between buy or sell orders. An order is related to a particular security and contains a quantity of shares, a type (limit or market) and, for limit orders, a limit price and a period of validity.

4.2.2. Order execution

The execution of the orders submitted by the traders is provided by the internal trading mechanism of the market. As seen in chapter 2, there are different mechanisms available such as CDA or CDAwMM. Given a certain trading mechanism, the market will try to match the order with the best available opposite order in the book of orders. The book of orders is the collection of all available orders at a given time.

4.2.3. Order confirmation

Once executed, the order should be confirmed to the trader. The most important information given to the trader in this process is the final transaction cost. Depending on the trading mechanism and the size of the order, the order execution could result in multiple transactions settled at different prices.

4.2.4. Transfer of share ownership

In a prediction market context, this action directly results from the order execution and is made at the same time. This mainly consists in transferring shares from one trader account to another.

4.2.5. Making payment

During the transfer of share ownership, the market also makes the appropriate payments or withdrawals based on the final transaction cost. The clearing house is responsible for guaranteeing enough liquidity for the withdrawal.

4.2.6. Securities quotations

The prediction market should also produce the necessary securities quotations to inform the traders of the market evolution. These quotations are based on the final transaction prices resulting from the orders' execution.

4.2.7. Basic account management

Under account management, we include the trader's identification, trader's authentication and opening and closing of accounts. These are basic features of electronic marketplaces.

4.2.8. Account endowment and guarantee

The account endowment is very particular to prediction markets and other play-money platforms. The goal of this endowment, as seen in section 2.7, is to provide initial liquidity in the form of cash and/or shares to the traders. The account guarantee, on the other hand, is a well-known mechanism in futures trading. It is managed by the clearing house in order to guarantee enough liquidity for short orders (a trader selling shares that he does not currently own).

4.2.9. Statements of account

The statements of account are the final component of prediction market platforms. They are the equivalent of the electronic or paper-based statements of account issued by traditional banks. It gives the trader the possibility of knowing, at any time, the exact value of its portfolio, as well as its history.

4.3. Electronic markets processes requirements

Kambil and van Heck [89] studied various forms of electronic markets, including prediction markets, and defined five trade processes and five trade context processes. These ten processes consist of the key processes underlying electronic trades. The first ones are required in all transactions of goods and services (search, valuation, logistics, payments and settlements, authentication) and the second ones are facilitators that help the course of the transaction (communications and computing, product representation, legitimation, influence and dispute resolution).

4.3.1. Search

This process supports buyers and sellers to identify opportunities. This results in the publication of real-time price information for each claim, as well as the current book of orders, in an open market.

4.3.2. Valuation (price negotiation)

This process supports the reaching of a price equilibrium through the buying and selling actions. This process could be supported by a market maker in order to guarantee a minimum liquidity on the market. Again, depending on the market settings, an open book of orders can provide useful advice on how to reach this equilibrium.

4.3.3. Logistics

This process specifies and coordinates the delivery of goods or services from sellers to buyers. In our case, this process presents no major challenge, all deliveries being supported by the marketplace and being mostly done for informational purposes.

4.3.4. Payment and settlements

This process ensures the settlement of payments. There are some key issues in this area. First, depending on the settings (short selling allowed), we should ensure that all traders have enough liquidity in order to process the payments at the settlement of the claims. This is traditionally supported by the clearing houses. Second, we have to ensure that all relevant information can be aggregated in the market, providing enough liquidity to the traders.

4.3.5. Authentication

This process covers a broad range of activities in the case of goods or services exchanges. In our context, this covers the authentication of the traders, strictly enforced or not, and the judgment of the claims at the settlement date.

4.3.6. Communications and computing

These processes support the operation of the marketplace. In our case, as everything is done electronically, this set of processes constitutes the core of the artifact.

4.3.7. Product representation

This process determines how the product attributes are presented to the traders. This consists of the claim definition and representation. A standardized process could help traders discover trading opportunities and thus improve the whole aggregating mechanism.

4.3.8. Legitimation

This process is used to validate the exchange agreement. This has little importance in our context, transactions being processed by the platform without interference of the traders.

4.3.9. Influence structures and processes

These processes implement mechanisms to enforce obligations. In our context, the main part is undertaken by the payment and settlements process, more precisely, by the clearing house. The second part of this process, the actions taken to enhance or create a good reputation, are part of the incentive mechanisms deployed to attract and retain the traders.

4.3.10. Dispute resolution

This process supports the resolution of disputes among parties. In our context, the disputes concern the judgment of the claims at their settlement date. An open process should guarantee to each trader access to the facts on which the settlement is based.

4.4. Requirements in a research community

Prediction markets are currently not widely deployed within R&D centers and universities, so we were unable to use existing literature to define the properties of a prediction market dedicated to research forecasting. In order to define the main characteristics of the platform, we carried out a series of six interviews with professors of the EPFL involved in the MICS project. These discussions enabled us to evaluate the difficulties which might be encountered when running this platform in the framework of a research project like MICS. They informed us of their reservations, but also gave us example claims which could be tested on such a market.

The outcome of these interviews is that in order to support the greatest possible interaction with the researchers, the prediction market must be (1) easy to use without prior knowledge of stock exchange mechanisms; (2) offer complete anonymity to the users; (3) restrict access to research community members and (4) carry out the transactions in an automated way, not requiring user intervention once the orders are submitted. From a more technical point of view, the market should be accessible at any time and any place by the project community while preventing access by external people.

4.4.1. Anonymity

For a research community, it is essential to guarantee the anonymity of both the transactions and the contents of the portfolio. This is required to avoid problems inside research teams as well as between them. Once successfully guaranteed, anonymity will enable the market to significantly aggregate information. Disclosure of the trader's identity during a transaction would either result in speculation based on the knowledge of a prominent actor instead of the knowledge of each individual trader at a time t, or in tensions between teams or researchers seeing their work undervalued by their peers. The same applies regarding the composition of the portfolios. The disclosure of their composition would allow every trader to precisely know the opinion of a particular trader regarding the chances of success of their own project or idea. This could lead to social strains or bias, traders being encouraged to compose their portfolio based on their superior beliefs or feeling disparaged by a colleague granting little interest to their project. In addition, anonymity protects the credibility of the traders who made poor predictions or predictions going against the mainstream.

Moreover, researches on the use of anonymity in group decision support systems (GDSS), show that groups working anonymously produce better results–in this case, decisions–than groups working without anonymity

[34]. Jessup et al. showed that in a GDSS context, anonymity reduce behavioral constraints on group members and led them to contribute more freely [87].

Thus, it is mainly for social reasons that the market will have to guarantee the complete anonymity of the traders. Anonymity is easy to integrate into such a platform and it could be compared with the relative anonymity granted on traditional stockmarkets.

4.4.2. Confidentiality

Two main issues regarding confidentiality were raised during the interviews: the guarantee of the intellectual property and the confidentiality of the internal evaluations as regards external (funding) partners.

Intellectual property Researchers are very cautious about sharing early research assumptions with others, and even more so when it is within a marketplace. Thus, to facilitate the emergence of new ideas, concepts or applications, it is imperative that the market should be restricted to members of the research community. However, to be introduced onto the market, a new claim will have to be precisely described, allowing its evaluation at settlement. This supposes, in many cases, a scientific publication accessible by everyone. It will thus be the responsibility of the user to decide what to reveal and what information to release onto the market, knowing that this information could be misused. Furthermore, describing an emerging research field in a marketplace is more sensible than publishing papers. Given the number of publications, these papers can be lost in the flood. Displayed in a marketplace, the new and promising research field suddenly gets more attention, maybe more than expected.

Backers The second issue regarding confidentiality is toward backers of the projects. Most of them already know the content of the projects, sometimes in a very complete way. The issue here is more towards the aggregated information available on the market. Researchers periodically give progress reports to their funding partners. These reports represent the official view of the project lead concerning a given research topic. Opening the prediction market information to these partners could change their view of the projects, resulting on unexpected consequences for their funding.

4.4.3. Contracts

The project management and researchers interest is more focused on the emergence of new ideas or applications than on the optimization of their own profit on the marketplace. Thus it is important that the submission process remain as easy as possible. For researchers, a prediction market must become one tool among others to test their ideas among their peers. Furthermore, the platform will have to integrate collaborative tools for discussion, allowing discussions regarding each claim, such as adding new (private) information or sharing doubt concerning its outcome. Filling this constraint, we can reasonably hope that the market would be able to act as an information aggregator within the community.

4.4.4. Trade

From an academic point of view it is obvious that the more ludic part–consisting of buying and selling shares according to information at the trader's disposal–will probably not motivate the majority of the researchers being active in the marketplace. For this reason, we will have to carefully design the trading process, allowing participants to spend as little time as possible to carry out their trades. Moreover, we should investigate alternative trading interfaces such as PDAs or mobile phones to enable the trading during presentations and seminars, allowing an immediate interaction with the market. Furthermore, we will have to pay attention to designing an adapted incentive mechanism. More information concerning the incentive mechanisms will be presented in section 5.5.4.

4.5. Interfaces and use cases

According to the needs and specifications detailed in the previous section, we can draw the principal use cases of a prediction market.

There is only one principal user type, the *trader*. Beside traders, we find two more user types: *visitors*—users without an account or users not yet authenticated—as well as *system administrators* (Figure 4.1). To pass from one status to the other, users have to authenticate themselves on the platform. Thus, all traders are also visitors, when they reach resources not requiring authentication.

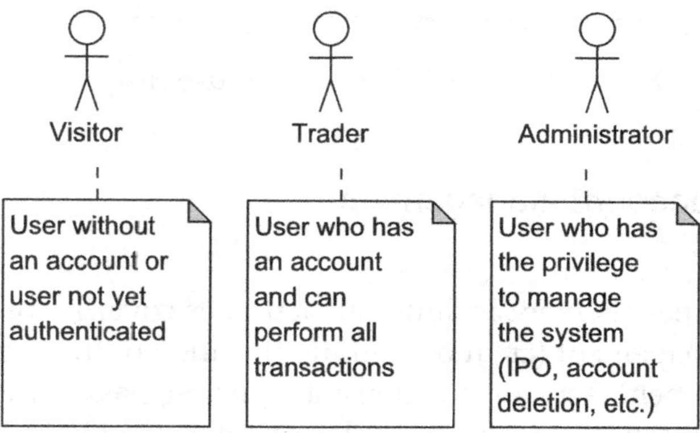

Figure 4.1.: Representation of the roles and their interdependence

The principal functions of the marketplace can be divided into four groups (Figure 4.2):

- user account management
- portfolio management
- claims management
- performance measurement

All other use cases could be deduced from their <<include>> or <<extend>> relations.

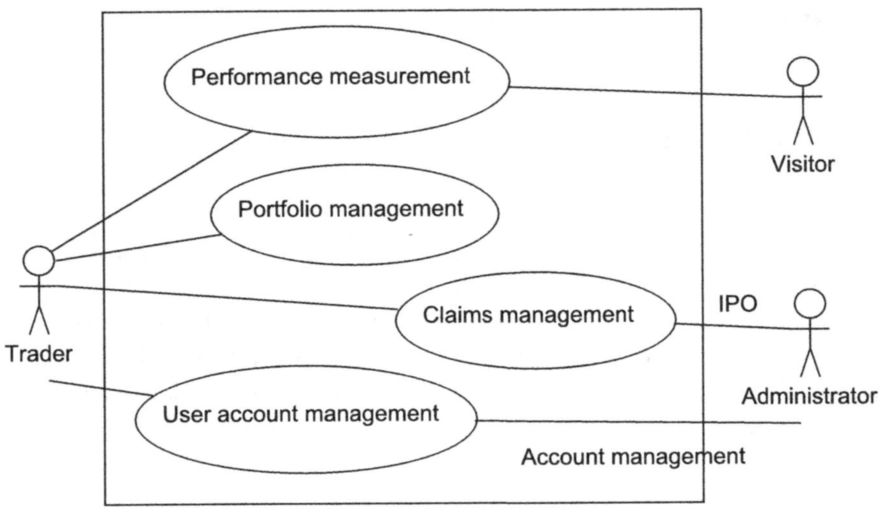

Figure 4.2.: MarMix principal use case

4.5.1. User account management

User account management includes all activities covering personal information management (creation and modification of the user profile), access management (account creation and deletion, password recovery) as well as information management (alarms, interesting links). All these activities are restricted to the trader type. Visitor type has access to account creation and password recovery.

4.5.2. Portfolio management

Portfolio management is the core of the system. This module supports the consultation of the account value (shares held and available cash) as well as trading by passing buy or sell orders. The trader is also able to consult the claims' quotes and to review his pending orders.

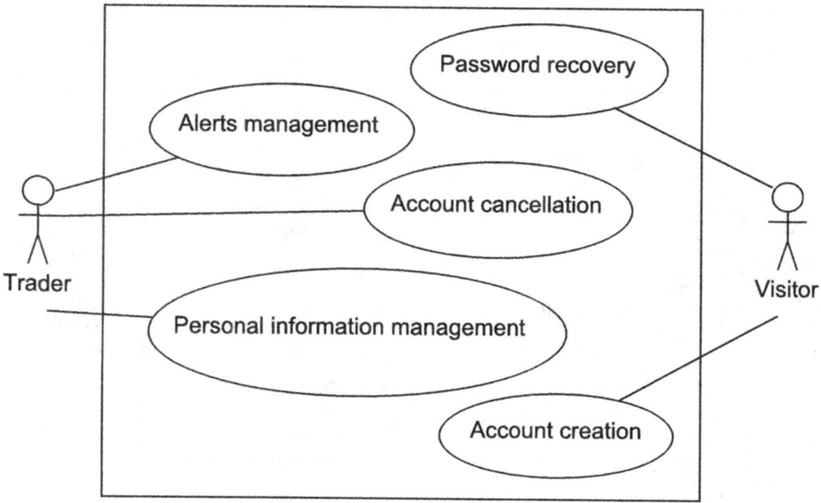

Figure 4.3.: User account management use case

Table 4.1.: User account management

Activity	Description
Account creation	Users can create a new personal account on the platform
Alerts management	Users can set and manage alerts based on the price of a given claim
Password recovery	Users can retrieve their password, sending it to the email address they used during the registration process
Personal information management	Users can edit the information they submitted during the registration process (username, real name, email address, etc.)
Account cancellation	Users can close their account and delete their personal information. Their past activities on the platform will remain available as past transaction cannot be deleted

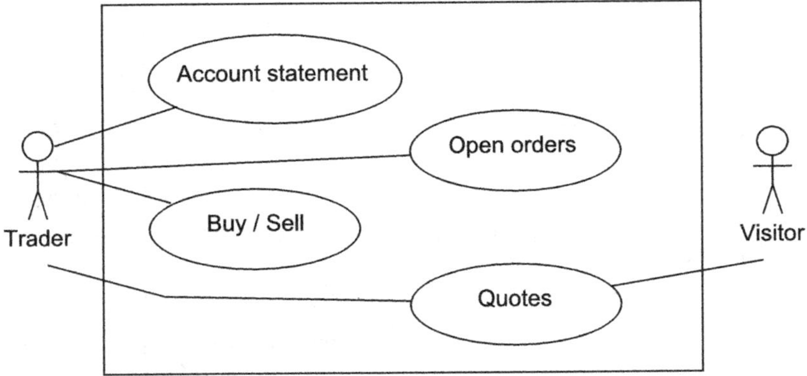

Figure 4.4.: Portfolio management use case

Table 4.2.: Portfolio management

Activity	Description
Account statement	Users can view their portfolio, their balance and the history of their wealth
Open orders	Users can review, edit or delete their open orders (mostly LIMIT orders)
Buy	Users can buy contracts of a given claim
Sell	Users can sell contracts of a given claim
Quotes	Users can view the various quotes and their history

4.5.3. Claims management

The claims management process is distributed between the trader submitting a new claim and the market administrator publishing the new claim on the market. The first one proposes a new claim and chooses its terms following an appropriate ontology as the second one is charged to formally accept the proposal before beginning the IPO process.

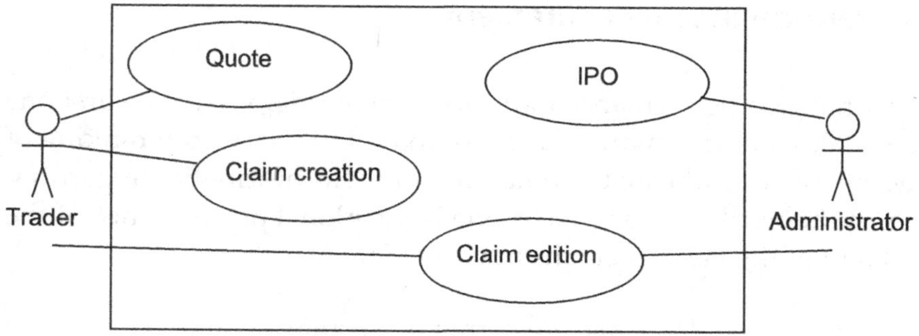

Figure 4.5.: Claims management use case

Table 4.3.: Claims management

Activity	Description
Quote	Users can view the quote of the claim and its history
Claim creation	Users can create a new claim based on a predefined template
Claim edition	Users can edit and review the claims they previously submitted and that are not yet published on the market
IPO	Users can start the IPO process, publishing the claim on the market

IPO process As soon as the new claim is published by the administrator, the status is changed to a new state, *Awaiting bids*. During this phase, the traders can place *LIMIT* orders on the claim. These orders are related to an auction, each trader indicating through their order their maximal belief in the outcome of the underlying claim. As soon as the orders' quorum is reached, the claim passes automatically in *Open* mode and becomes available for all traders and all orders' types—limit or market.

4.5.4. Performance measurement

The user has two performance indicators at their disposal. The first one is their ranking on the marketplace compared to the overall ranking of all traders, which indicate the reliability of their information regarding claims on the market. The second one is the global performance of the market and of the various claims in particular.

Table 4.4.: Performance display

Activity	**Description**
Users' ranking	Users can view their overall ranking on the platform, based on their past performance
Market's performance	Users can view and compare the market's performance with their own one
Claim's performance	Users can view the performance of a given claim

4.6. Internal software architecture

In this section, we will describe some significant sequence diagrams issued from the uses cases presented in section 4.5. These diagrams illustrate the interaction between the trader and the marketplace. They

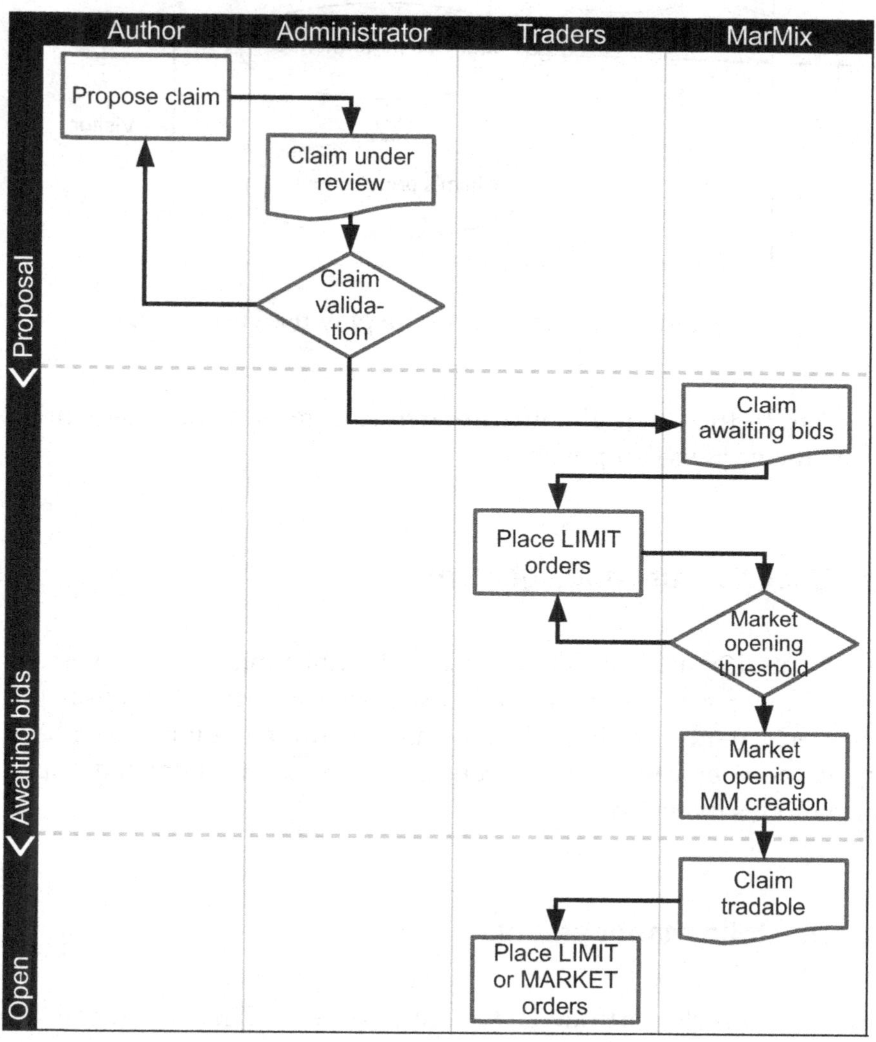

Figure 4.6.: IPO process

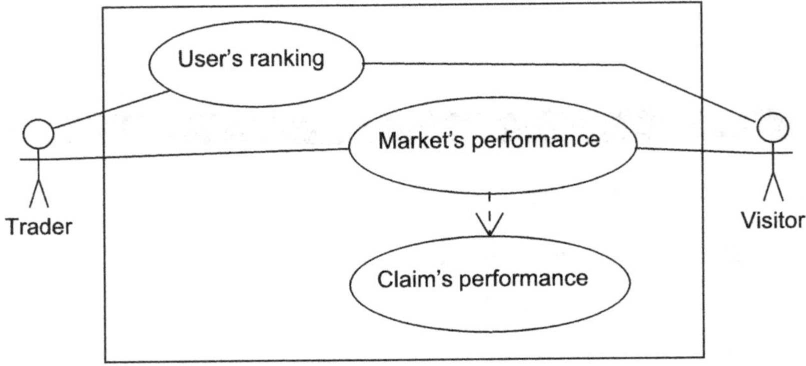

Figure 4.7.: Performance display use case

also illustrate the internal software architecture and the interactions between the various components.

4.6.1. User account management

Using the mod_apache_auth module to authenticating users, register.py receives the necessary information to create the new user account from the web server. After reviewing this information and making the necessary changes, the user validates their entry. The account is created and a confirmation is issued to the user.

4.6.2. Portfolio management

Displaying a user's portfolio is done in two steps. First, we get all the claims owned by the trader, as for a traditional account statement. This gives us the claims and the quantity owned. For each of them, we then collect the current quotes and the general terms of the claim. As a result, the trader gets a list with all claims, their properties and their current price.

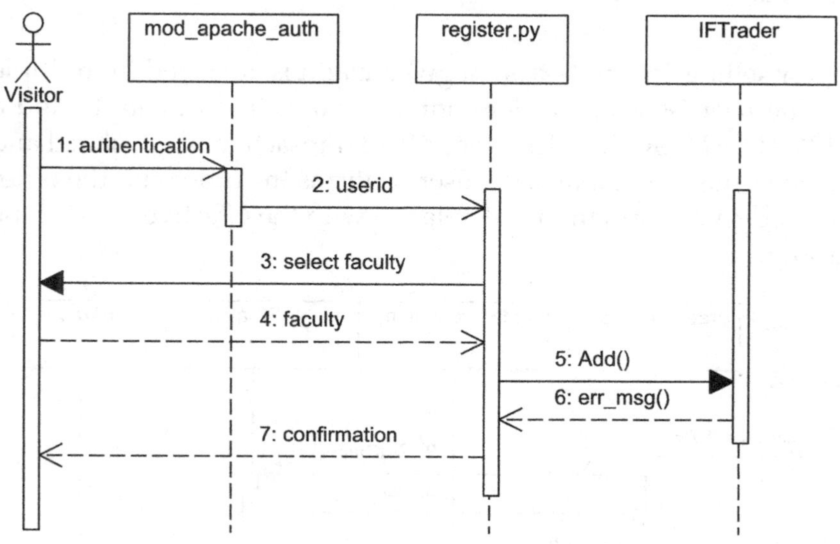

Figure 4.8.: User account management sequence diagram

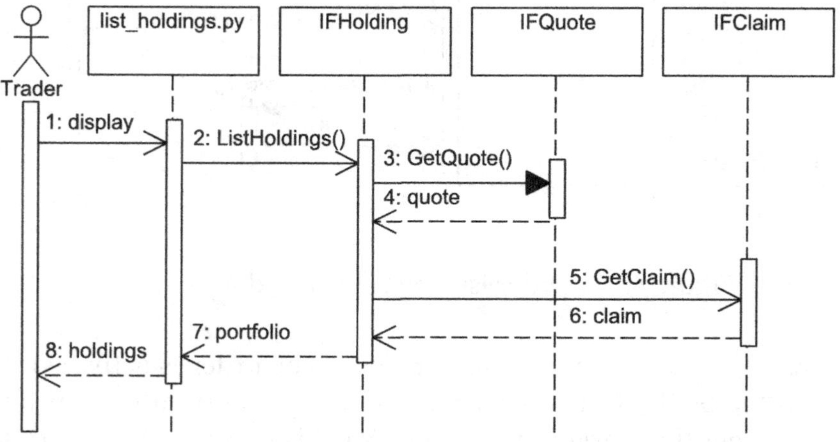

Figure 4.9.: Portfolio management sequence diagram

4.6.3. Order issuing

Buying or selling contracts from a given claim is achieved in multiple steps. The user issues an order containing a claim, a quantity and a type (LIMIT or MARKET). The price of the transaction is calculated and displayed to the user. Finally, the user confirms the order and the order is processed. A confirmation is displayed with the effective price of the transaction.

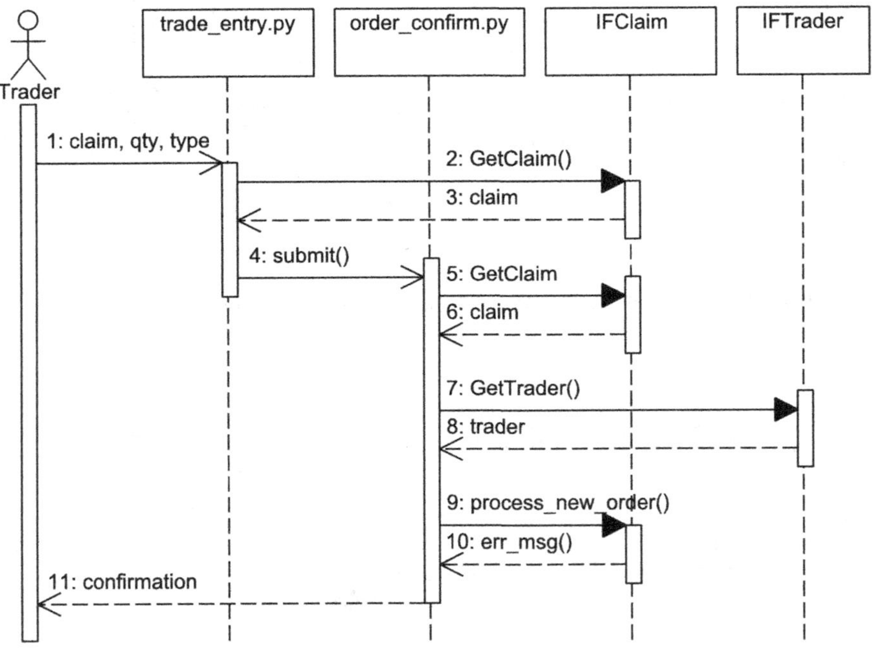

Figure 4.10.: Order issuing sequence diagram

The transaction itself is a complex process. The order is activated, to appear in the book of orders. If the claim is not currently in an IPO process, we get the market maker offer for this order. Then we try to match the order with orders already in the book of orders or with the market maker offer. When the matching is done, we update the price function of the market maker and the quote. Finally, we update the portfolio of the trader.

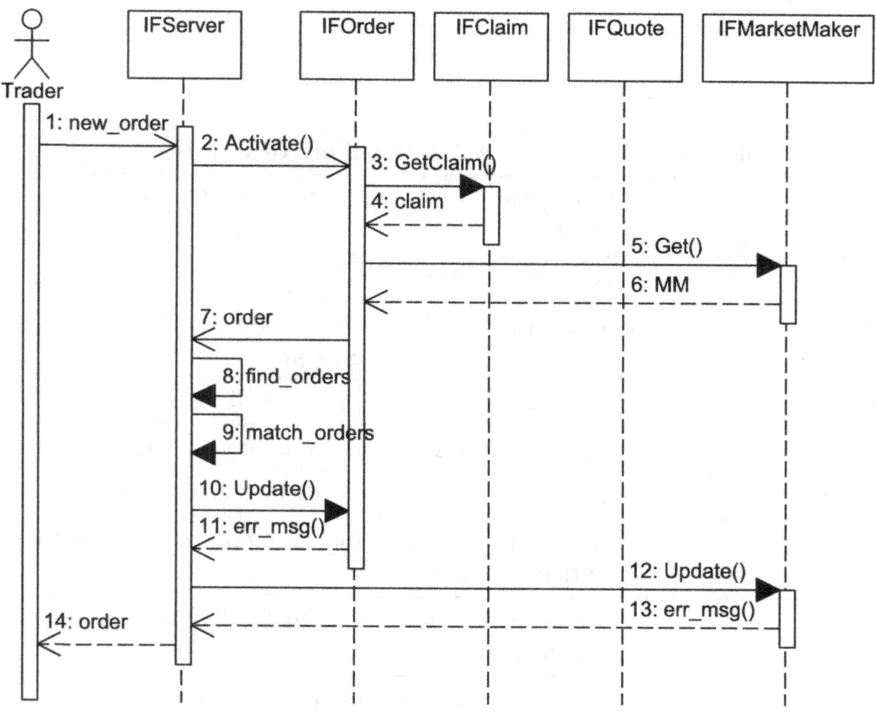

Figure 4.11.: Order transaction sequence diagram

4.6.4. Claim management

The two main parts of this process are the creation of the claim and its IPO. Most public prediction markets use very basic claim descriptions mostly based on the schema: "Will X append before t". Even if this scheme could conduct to unsettable claims or could lead to dispute concerning the settlement, it could satisfy most basic requirements. In order to support complex claims, we need an improved claim description. We will describe, in depth, our results in section 5.5.1, but we can already present some constitutive parts of a claim description in Table 4.5.

Table 4.5.: Constitutive parts of a claim description

Symbol	The symbol of the claim that will be displayed in the market
Name	A carefully selected wording that presents the claim
Author	The author of the claim or a person who could explain the terms if necessary
Type	The underlying prediction type (binary, index, etc.)
Project	The project from which the claim is issued
Settle date	The settlement date (defined or undefined)
Jury	Who will determine the status of the claim at the settlement date
Source	The source of information that will be used to settle the claim
Price	The price range (usually from 0 to 100)
Payment	How the final payment will be calculated
Field of research	The research fields from which this claim is issued
State of the art	Some results obtained in the research fields regarding this claim
Expected results	The propositions that will be validated if this claim succeed
Measure of success	The indicators and their values that will be used to determine the claim's settlement

We will see in section 5.5.1 that these descriptions can be adapted based on the context and on the assessment goal.

The following diagram contains all actions linked to the publication of a new claim and its IPO process. It includes the creation of a claim, its edition, the opening of the market and the creation of the market maker.

Sequence 1 to 10 consists of entering a new symbol and creating a contract using propose.py. As we saw (Figure 4.12), the administrator must then validate the contract and put it in mode AWAITING_BIDS (11–14). From this point, the users can pass LIMIT orders until the threshold quantity is reached (15–20). As soon as the threshold is reached, the opening of the market begins. The wallets are upgraded (22–27) and the market maker is created (28–35). Finally, the user receives the confirmation that the order was correctly passed and that the market is open.

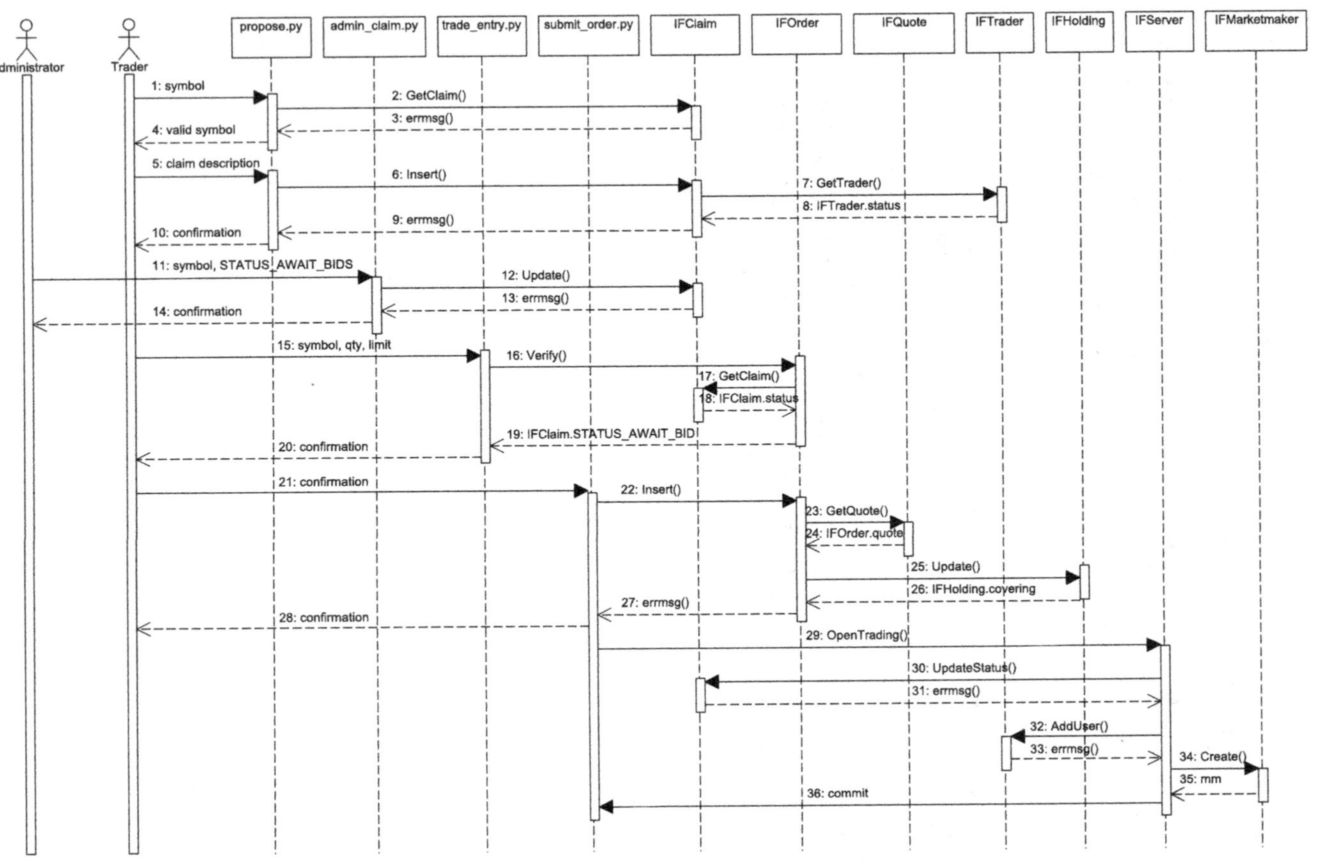

Figure 4.12.: Claim management sequence diagram

4.6.5. Performance measurement

User ranking is done at regular intervals via a cron job which upgrades the values of the table account_history. The value returned by ComputeReturn() is issued by the table account_history.

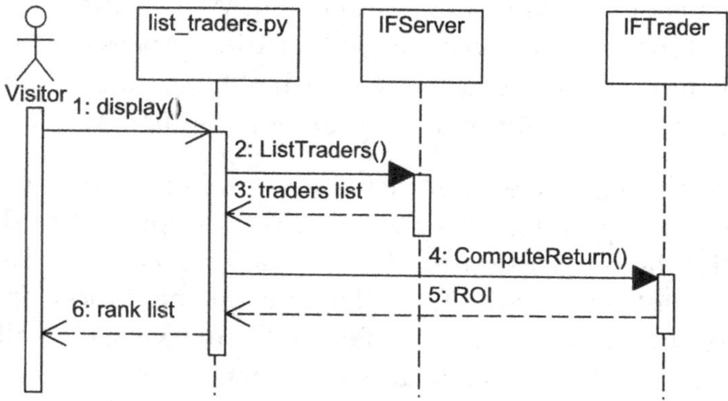

Figure 4.13.: Performance measurement process

4.7. Design factors

During our literature review, we identified many design factors that should be considered to design a prediction market. Thus, there is currently no study identifying these factors and testing them against the outcome of the market.

Some authors attempt to identify all or parts of these factors. Currently, the most complete contribution is the one of LaComb et al. [97] about their implementation of the Imagination Market at GE.

Many laboratory studies dealt with the financial and economic design of these markets and tested their outcome, but–with some exceptions–never dealt with the overall design of these markets.

Our aim here is not to cover the extensive laboratory experiments and their outcomes. This was dealt with in section 2.8. It is more to identify the main design factors and their various implementations in known field studies and—if available—their impact on the overall performance of the platform.

We identified 30 different design factors summarised in Table 4.7. Some of them are independent and others are dependent. We then made four main categories: (1) incentive mechanisms, (2) trading process, (3) investor management and (4) clearing house. For each of these main components, we then itemized each factor with more or less granularity.

This itemization made, we constructed an ontology with our design factors. The first step of this construction was to supply a shared framework to assist the design of a prediction market. The next step was to define different sets of rules for different implementations (political markets, sport markets, ideation markets, R&D markets, etc.) allowing the derivation of a set of design factors with their settings relative to the chosen implementation.

Following the itemization, we defined for each design factor their characteristics and their possible settings.

4.7.1. Incentive mechanisms

The incentive mechanism provides motivation to participants to actively be involved with the platform. There are three main components: (1) performance evaluation and measurement, (2) rewards and (3) involvement. Several studies [107, 147, 151, 85] discussed various incentive schemes, but none of them proposed a set of working mechanisms. This is mainly due to the fact that each market configuration and organization type need an adapted incentive scheme [147].

However, Wolfers and Zitzewitz [171] show the importance of a robust incentive mechanism. This mechanism should motivate participants to be involved on the market, as well as to share their own private information with the market.

Table 4.6.: Prediction market design factors

Incentive mechanisms	Performance	Performance evaluation	Wealth: portfolio value based Accuracy: best predictors Effort: trading behavior[a]
		Performance measurement	Last trading price VWAP[b] Specific algorithm
	Reward	Reward type	Non-monetary (prize) Monetary Corporate support[c]
		Reward base	Tournament: performance based Lottery: luck based
	Involvement		Trading sessions Workshops Trainings Other involvement techniques
Trading process	Fees		Trading fees Expiration fees IPO fees
	Trading mechanisms	Double auction	Open order book Closed order book
		Market maker	MSR DPM CDAwMM
	Trading time		24/7 Trading sessions Selected opening hours

[a] A fixed number of trades required to participate
[b] VWAP: Volume weighted average price
[c] Project funding, team funding, resources for idea development

Table 4.7.: Prediction market design factors (Continued)

Clearing house	Order	Order matching rules	Price and submission Price and quantity
		Order spending caps	Enforced No caps
		Order type	Market Limit
		Short selling	Allowed Not allowed
	Asset	Asset type	Real money Play-money
		Inflation	Play-money only
		Borrowing	Margin purchases
		Endowment	Initial endowment (money and/or contracts) Weekly endowment (money and/or contracts)
	Claim	Claim IPO	Fees and rewards Screening[d]
		Initial claims	Starting quotes Quantity
		Claim ontology	
		Claim type	Winner-take-all[e] Conditional Index Spread
		Claim structure	Bundle[f] Independent
	Payoff	Settlement date	Public Random
		Settlement judge	
		Settlement price	"Truth" (if available) Proxy measure (expert, objective value, etc.) VWAP Final market price

[d] Screening by experts or by the market
[e] Also called Arrow-Debreu
[f] Mutually exclusive or multiple outcome

Table 4.8.: Prediction market design factors (Continued)

Investor management	Market	Market policy	Open market Closed market
		Market transparency	Display all information Restrict to some indicators
	Investor	Investor anonymity	User ID Username No anonymity
		Investor unicity	Enforced (LDAP, ...) Trust
		Investor selection	Quantity Diversity Informed vs non-informed Benefit from the outcome of the market

Performance

As we will see later, the performance could be or not be used to reward the participants. Thus, to situate themselves on the market, traders need some comparison indicators.

Performance evaluation When talking about performance in this context, it is generally supposed that the performance is based on the actual *wealth* of the participants. This assertion supposes that the current value of the portfolio represent the participant's capabilities to accurately predict the outcome of the markets. This is not quite true. It represents the ability of the trader to take advantage of the market fluctuations. Moreover, on long-running prediction markets, especially if weekly endowments are paid, this could just be an indicator of the duration of the trader's participation.

Dahan [38] proposes to use other evaluations like *accuracy*—the percentage of accurate predictions made by the trader—or *effort*—the trading behavior of the trader in terms of the number of transactions, the intensity of participation or the number of new claims submitted.

Performance measurement The measurement of performance is the way we compute the performance indicator. It is linked to performance evaluation, each different evaluation basis implying another measure. In the case of a measurement based on the wealth of the trader, the most common measure is the sum of the *payoff* of the different claims. Thus LaComb et al. [96] tried to use a scheme for calculating the payoff that was different from the one for calculating performance, due to technical reasons, which led to confusion between the traders.

For other evaluation schemes, we will have to define a way to measure performance and to explain it carefully to the participants.

Reward

For Wolfers and Zitzewitz [171], "even well-designed markets will fail unless a motivation to trade exists". It is also agreed that it is more difficult to motivate traders to participate in a corporate prediction market than in a "for fun" public prediction market.

Reward type We identified three types of reward: (1) monetary rewards—induced by using real-money liquidity, (2) non monetary rewards—generally prizes, and (3) corporate support—funding of teams, projects or personal evaluation.

As we will see later, there is no proof that monetary rewards—playing with real-money—led to better predictions. Moreover, given the legal restrictions on using real money [10], we will not further develop this type of reward.

Prizes seem to provide good motivation as seen in various studies [157, 27, 147]. Furthermore, they are compatible with most organizations' policies. Prizes could be vouchers, gadgets, electronic devices, trips, etc.

In a corporate environment, we should also study the opportunity of using corporate support as reward. This could be linked to the traded claim in the form of the allocation of resources to pursue the idea. This also could be linked to business units or teams, allocating more resources given the team's performances. Finally, this could be taken into account during the annual performance evaluation of the participant.

Reward base Given the choice of one or more reward type, we should now decide on what basis to give the reward. The two main bases are the tournament and the lottery.

A tournament-based reward is given to the best traders, given the performance measure defined previously while a lottery-based reward randomly selects the traders to be rewarded. We can also reduce the number of participants taking part in the lottery, by selecting only the best traders. In this case, we have a performance-based lottery.

There are currently not many results concerning these two rewarding bases. However, James and Isaac [86] show that "repeated, shared trading experience when tournament incentives are in place promotes divergence from intrinsic value pricing". Furthermore, Luckner [107] studied the incidence of various payment schemes on the performance of the markets and found that "performance-compatible payment schemes seem to perform worse than fixed payments and the rank-order tournament".

Involvement

Unlike public prediction markets, enterprise markets can use various involvement schemes to commit the participant to trade on the market. LaComb et al. [96] used various schemes such as group trading sessions, workshops or training sessions. Siegel [147] and Soukhoroukova et al. [154] extended these schemes with methods such as reports on the corporate intranet or meetings with executives.

4.7.2. Trading process

There are three considerations to take into account regarding the trading process. First of all, the *trading mechanism*, which is the heart of the platform and determines how the trades will be made on the market. Directly related, we should determine the *trading fees* and the *trading time*.

Trading fees

To our knowledge, there are no experiments exploring the effects of trading fees on the accuracy of the market. Some real-money or play-money public prediction markets are charging fees on transactions [1] but the majority of the platform do not. If enabled, one will have to decide to which transactions fees will be applied. This could be, for example, a transaction fee on orders, on the settlement of the claim or on the process of submitting a new claim on the market.

Trading mechanisms

Many trading mechanisms are available on prediction market platforms. We distinguish two main categories, with or without an automated market maker. All mechanisms have been exhaustively tested in various experiments.

Double auction Probably the easiest to set up, the double auction mechanism is used on multiple platforms [145, 171, 65]. It is the mechanism driving the majority of the stock exchanges such as NYSE and AMEX.

One should also choose the way to deal with the order book. The most common implementation is the *open order book*. [3] proposes the use of the

1. For example, Intrade (`http://www.intrade.com`) or HSX (`http://www.hsx.ch`)

closed order book to reduce traders' insight into policy markets. Baruch [7] shows "that, on average, prices in an open-book environment are more informative".

Market maker Automated market makers have been heavily studied in the prediction market literature [1, 12, 81, 71, 75, 99, 126, 163] and are known to bring additional liquidity to the marketplace, increasing the accuracy of the market. Furthermore, they are an additional way to motivate traders, allowing them to pass orders as they like, without waiting for corresponding orders.

The most famous is Hanson's Market Scoring Rules (MSR) [75]. It is widely implemented in prediction market software [2]. A combination of MSR and CDA was proposed by Hanson [71] and then successfully implemented in various software too [3].

Pennock [126] proposes another implementation based on horse race betting, the Dynamic Pari-Mutuel (DPM). The DPM algorithm is not much discussed, but was implemented in Yahoo! Tech Buzz Game [4].

Trading time

Large public prediction markets are almost open 24/7. For various reasons some market close for one hour each day [5]. On the other hand, most experiments restrict the timeframe in which the traders can be active [27, 96, 133].

The main issue is keeping the traders engaged and generating enough trades to properly aggregate trader's private information.

2. Prediction market software implementing an MSR automated market maker: InklingMarkets (http://www.inklingmarkets.com/), CrowdCast (http://www.crowdcast.com/), Wisdom Hive (http://www.wisdomhive.com/), Ask Markets (http://www.askmarkets.com/), Microsoft PredictionPoint (http://www.microsoft.com/)

3. Prediction market software implementing an MSR automated market maker with a CDA: Zocalo (http://zocalo.sourceforge.net/), Nosco (http://www.nosco.dk/)

4. The Tech Buzz Game is now closed (http://research.yahoo.com/node/2359)

5. This is, for example, the case with Intrade (http://www.intrade.com/)

4.7.3. Investor management

Traders are the main element of the marketplace. Currently there are not many studies dealing with design factors about the traders. Some researchers are analyzing the accuracy of the markets in regard to the number of active traders. It is agreed that a large community of traders has a positive impact on prediction market results [15]. However, Christiansen [33] and Plott and Chen [133] showed that small markets were also able to run effectively. Christiansen [33] showed the importance of the ratio of claims to traders.

Market

Market factors often result from organizational considerations. This is true for both market policy and market transparency.

Market policy By their very nature, public prediction markets are *open markets* and most corporate markets are *closed markets*. Gruca et al. [65] show "that open markets do a better job of prediction than closed markets" but could not identify the main reason for this performance difference (greater dispersion of information, greater liquidity or better informed traders).

Market transparency Normally prediction markets give traders all the available information and let them effectively aggregate their beliefs. Thus, in certain configurations, one would want to reduce the available information to a subset of all available information. This could be the case in public policy and decision markets [77].

Investor

When there are no restrictions due to the confidentiality of the claims traded, more traders and greater diversity of traders would lead to more accurate predictions. This is due to the automatic weighting of each trader's influence on the market regarding their wealth.

Investor anonymity As discussed earlier, anonymity is a real issue on prediction markets. Hanson [78] shows that "secret accounts, trader anonymity, and complex shared interests, however, might conspire to make it difficult for advisors to reveal credibly their relevant holdings". Thus the large majority of all experiments made guarantee the anonymity of traders.

Investor unicity Unicity of the traders accounts could become a problem in anonymous markets and be used to manipulate the market [91]. However, in an enterprise context, one could easily exclude this risk by linking the prediction market to the enterprise authentication infrastructure.

Investor selection Even if the markets are very efficient at aggregating information, they cannot aggregate more information than is submitted by the traders. For this reason, one should carefully select the participants playing on the market. As said earlier, the more the better. Thus if it is not possible for various reasons, one has to pay attention, allowing enough uninformed traders to participate in order to provide incentive for the better informed traders to release private information [172].

4.7.4. Clearing house

"A clearing house is a financial services company that provides clearing and settlement services for financial transactions, usually on a futures exchange, and often acts as central counterparty (the payor actually pays the clearing house, which then pays the payee). A clearing house may also offer novation, the substitution of a new contract or debt for an old, or other credit enhancement services to its members."[6]

This definition does not exactly correspond to our implementation, which is broader, but it gives a good idea of the function of a clearing house. For this reason, one should not take the term "clearing house" in too strict a sense.

Order

This is the heart of the platform. It defines the main characteristics of the transactions.

Order matching rules There are currently two established matching rules driving most CDA stock exchanges, the *price–time priority* and the *price–size priority*[7].

The price–time priority matches the orders by first sorting them by price and then by their time of entry. Priority is given to the oldest orders.

The price–quantity priority matches the orders by first sorting them by price and then by quantity. Priority is given to the smallest orders. As stated by LaComb et al. [97], the Foresight Exchange use a reverse price–quantity matching rule, giving the priority to large orders.

Order spending caps By default, traders are allowed to spend all their money in shares, related to their beliefs. One could decide to place spending caps on amounts spent or on the number of same shares possessed. This could be necessary to prevent market manipulation in play-money marketplaces [2]. However, the large majority of the prediction markets do not enforce spending caps.

6. Wikipedia, retrieved June 22, 2009 (http://en.wikipedia.org/wiki/Clearing_house_(finance))

7. For example, see the "Matching Rules for the order driven part of the Exchange System" published by the Swiss Exchange (SWX) (http://www.six-swiss-exchange.com/download/trading/training/3_match_en.pdf)

Order type The orders type depends on the chosen market mechanism. In the case of a CDA market, only *limit* orders are allowed. Using a market maker, one could implement *market* orders. And in the case of a CDAwMM, one could implement both, *limit* and *market* orders. But in CDAwMM, one should pay attention to clearly informing the traders on the differences between the two types of order.

In the case of *limit* orders—combined or not with *market* orders—one could also define an order expiry value. Thus, after a given timeframe, the orders are automatically deleted.

Short selling Short selling—the ability to sell shares that the trader does not possess—is implemented in prediction market software. Chan et al. [27], Gruca et al. [66] and Spears et al. [157] restricted short selling in their experiments for various reasons. Spears et al. [157] "removed short selling since earlier participants had found it to be confusing".

Thus, it seems that constraints on short selling could lead to speculative bubbles [171], though even Noeth et al. [116] assert that "removing the short selling restriction does not improve information aggregation".

Asset

There are two different types of assets: *play-money* and *real-money*. Currently, the large majority of the prediction markets are based on play-money, with the exception of the Iowa Electronic Market (IEM)[8] and Intrade[9].

Asset type Since 2004 several studies have tried to compare the incidence of *play-money* or *real money* on the outcomes of prediction markets [140, 146, 151]. Currently, they shows that a reward mechanism is necessary to guarantee market accuracy, but could not prove that real money

8. `http://www.biz.uiowa.edu/iem/`
9. `http://www.intrade.com/`

led to better accuracy than prize-based rewards. Moreover, there are some important issues using real money prediction markets [10].

Using play-money on the platform, one should define the settings of the three following factors: *inflation*, *borrowing* and *endowment*.

Play-money inflation We found an interesting quote from LaComb et al. [97] proposing to introduce inflation to "increase liquidity in the market by penalizing participants who sit on cash". However, this should be more deeply investigated.

Play-money borrowing Here again, this is a new idea from LaComb et al. [97] and should be further investigated. The reason allowing borrowing play-money from the market is to provide similar functionality to that of traditional markets. However, this could lead to inaccurate predictions, traders having lost their cash in poor predictions would exert too much weight on the market if they are allowed to borrow more money.

Play-money endowment As the traders are not putting their own money on the market—as in real-money markets—we should endow them in order for them to be able to play. The endowment could takes place at the beginning of the play—or during account creation—and in certain cases, weekly or monthly during the game.

Even if Seemann et al. [144] showed "that the stock endowments significantly foster liquidity in the market", we found that most play-money markets use exclusively play-money endowments.

The allocation of stocks could therefore solve the issue raised by LaComb et al., concerning traders sitting on their cash, by forcing them to make transactions in order to achieve a balanced portfolio.

Regarding current experiments [6], it seems that a mix of shares and cash could lead to the best results. However, there are currently no studies concerning the perfect mix.

Finally one should consider weekly or monthly endowments if there are long-term claims on the market. Traders will not recover liquidity to trade on new claims before the settlement of their current claims, forcing them to liquidate positions whereas information in their possession did not change.

Claim

Claims are defined by the market purpose. It should be clearly defined in order to be able to correctly describe the various claims.

Claim IPO The IPO process allows traders, but also the market owner, to add new shares onto the market. The goals of this process are: (1) to attract new ideas or information from the traders and (2) to keep the traders interested by regularly publishing new claims.

We discussed a proposition for an IPO process in [55]. There are currently different implementations of this process, relying on the same basis [154].

The first step is the *screening*. One should decide whether the claims are to pass through a screening process run by *experts*—some players, executives, field experts—or made by the *market*—all players are allowed to place orders till the predefined threshold is reached. This threshold is commonly a quantity of orders or shares.

The initial price could be *fixed* by the experts or be a *uniform price* for each IPO, or could depend on the auctions during the IPO, resulting in a *variable price*.

We have summarized these different possibilities in Table 4.7.4.

Initial claims Siegel [147] and Wolfers and Zitzewitz [171] assert that the initial claims—in the case of an ideation market—should be sticky enough to attract the traders. Therefore, one should pay attention to

Table 4.9.: Different IPO matrix

Screening	Price	Fees
Experts	Uniform	Flat[a] No
	Variable	Variable[b] No
Market	Uniform	Flat[a] No
	Variable	Variable[b] No

[a] Flat fees are fixed by the marketplace
[b] Variable fees are defined as a fraction of the IPO value

putting enough interesting claims at the launch of the marketplace. More claims may be added during the game, but discouraged traders will probably never come back.

Depending on the experiments, the number of claims initially published on the market varies from 5 to 10.

Claim ontology Badly worded claims are a real issue in our context. Hanson [73] wrote that "even if an issue becomes settled, a poorly worded claim on that issue may be unresolvable. To avoid this, we need techniques for avoiding ambiguity and incentives for players to use them". Therefore, we propose to use a claim ontology to help traders to better word their claims.

Claim type There are currently four different types of claims commonly used on prediction markets. Their utilization depends on the underlying outcome (Table 4.7.4).

Table 4.10.: Four claim types and their utilization

Type	Description	Example	Outcome y
Winner-take-all[a]	Contract pays 1 if event occurs, 0 otherwise	Product x will be available on June 30	Probability that event y occurs
Conditional	Contract pays 1 if event occurs and z is True, 0 otherwise	Product x will be available on June 30, and will integrate the component z	Combinatorial probability that event y occurs
Index	Contract pays 1 for each percent of y	Market share y of product x on June 30	Mean value of outcome y
Spread	Contract pays 2 if the threshold y is exceeded	Market share of product x will exceed y on June 30	Median value of y

[a] Also called Arrow-Debreu

Claim structure Given the selected outcomes, the claims could be bundled in *mutually exclusive* or *multiple outcome* bundle. *Mutually exclusive* claims are based on two or more binary claims assembled in a portfolio. This is the case, for example, if we want to predict which product model will make the biggest sales during one month. *Multiple outcome* bundle could be used with index or binary claims. At the settlement, more than one claim will be selected. This could be used, for example, to select the three best ideas out of ten.

Payoff

The *payoff* factors define the way one settles the claim, as well at the settlement price.

Settlement date On markets with outcomes bound to an end date, such as the winner of an election, we should use this date as the settlement date. Otherwise, with the outcome not bound to an end date, as on ideation or new product markets, one could adopt one of two different strategies. The first, as in prediction markets applied to political elections, is to define the settlement date at the claim's creation. The second to avoid speculation preceding market close by choosing a random closing date [92].

Settlement judge The judge is charged with settling the claim based on the defined judging rules. These rules should be carefully written in order to restrict interpretation issues. Markets not relying on concrete settlement rules, such as ideation markets, should simply settle the claims based on the payoff function. Recently Intrade had a lot of trouble regarding the settlement of a claim on whether North Korea would, by July 31, 2006, successfully fire ballistic missiles that would land outside its airspace. They defined, in advance, the DoD as the judging source, which made no comment on the July 5 test whereas other US government source did.

Settlement price In the case of claims that could be settled regarding concrete facts, the payoff depends on the claim's type. The payoff is then $1 if True and $0 otherwise for a winner-take-all claim.

In other cases, it is more difficult to choose a payoff function to mitigate the manipulation risks. Even if it is agreed that the market closing price is a good payoff for prediction markets, some experiments have tried other payoff functions. Soukhoroukova et al. [154] used proxies—in this case, experts—to define the payoff for each claim depending on their own appreciation. This led to some trouble between the traders and the experts regarding the final evaluation. In other context, the proxy payoff function could be successfully used, relying on concrete and verifiable facts such as market shares, number of sales, movie visitors, etc. LaComb et al. [96] used a VWAP over the last five trading day, to mitigate the risk that traders tried to made last minute profits.

4.8. MarMix artifact

The implementation of MarMix was based only on free software, partly by interest of the author, and partly to enable other people to take on all or part of the project and carry on the development.

In order to accelerate the development of the prototype, it was decided to base MarMix on an existing development. At the start of this work, only three software packages were available under a free license: Ideosphere which is based on a succession of Perl scripts and which is used daily in the Ideosphere marketplace; USIFEX, which is based on Python scripts and has not been used since the beginning of 2000; and finally FreeMarket which is written in PHP and is based on a MySQL database.

4.8.1. Typology of the MarMix artifact

Based on our typology of design factors, we derived the requirements for our MarMix artifact. The resulting design factors are presented in Table 4.8.1. Our goal was to design our prediction market in the simplest way, omitting all factors that might unnecessarily raise the complexity of the software. Moreover, we also made design choices to follow, as much as possible, real futures exchanges due to the lack of knowledge of non-real-life-like setups.

Table 4.11.: MarMix design factors

Incentive mechanisms	Performance	Performance evaluation	Wealth: portfolio-value based
		Performance measurement	Last trading price
	Reward	Reward type	Non-monetary (prize)
		Reward base	Tournament: performance-based
	Involvement		Trading sessions
Trading process	Fees		No fees
	Trading mechanisms	Double auction	Open order book
		Market maker	CDAwMM
	Trading time		24/7
Investor management	Market	Market policy	Closed market
		Market transparency	Display all information
	Investor	Investor anonymity	Username
		Investor unicity	Enforced (Switch AAI)[a]
		Investor selection	All project members

[a] Swiss Universities Authentication and Authorization Infrastructure

Table 4.12.: MarMix design factors (Continued)

Clearing house	Order	Order matching rules	Price and submission
		Order spending caps	No caps
		Order type	Market and limit
		Short selling	Allowed
	Asset	Asset type	Play-money
		Inflation	No
		Borrowing	Yes
		Endowment	Initial endowment: Play-money
	Claim	Claim IPO	Fees and rewards: No Screening: Only for the wording
		Initial claims	Starting quotes: IPO Quantity: 5
		Claim ontology	Enforced for claim's proposals
		Claim type	Winner-take-all[b]
		Claim structure	Independent
	Payoff	Settlement date	Public
		Settlement judge	Claim owner
		Settlement price	Final market price

[b] Also called Arrow-Debreu

Incentive mechanisms

During the design of MarMix we had little knowledge of the difficulties of motivating traders to play on the platform, so we chose very simple settings for these factors. Given the organization of our environment we planned trading sessions during conference breaks and dedicated workshops.

Trading process

Resulting from our interviews, we choose to use a market maker with 24/7 trading time to allow traders to pass orders at any time and to receive instant feedback from the market. This setup allows a continuous aggregation of new information.

Investor management

The running context at our disposal drove our design choices. These choices are mainly a transparent closed market restricted to traders, authenticated by a central repository.

Clearing house

Given our academic context and the difficulties of using real money on the platform, we chose to implement play-money. We also made design choices to follow as much as possible real futures exchanges. This implies the ability to sell short, to allow borrowing and to support a full IPO process. Moreover, we used traditional settlement with a public closing date.

4.8.2. Choice of software

For the author, beside supporting most of our requirements, the software selection criteria were the following:

- licensed under free software (GPL or related license) to allow code changes and free distribution;
- running on a GNU/Linux server;
- object-oriented programming to facilitate the maintenance and development of the platform;
- based on a database to allow various kinds of reporting;
- good documentation of the code;
- complete separation of logic and presentation.

We made a comparison of the different platforms and decided to use USIFEX as the basis for our prototype. Despite the fact that it lacks good documentation, it has more functionality than Ideosphere. This also involved a lot of work in upgrading the code, made necessary by the age of the code (5 years) and the new versions as well of Python of as PostgreSQL.

Table 4.13.: Comparison of the free prediction markets software[a]

Criteria	Ideosphere	USIFEX	FreeMarket	Zocalo
License	IFPL[b]	Mozilla	BSD	MIT
Language	Perl 5	Python 2.1	PHP 4	Java
Database	Text file	PostgreSQL	MySQL	Hibernate
Programming	Object	Object	Procedural	Object
Code documentation	Very good	Poor	None	Very good
Separation Logic/presentation	Complete	Complete	None	Complete
Installation	Confirmed user	Expert	Beginner	Beginner
Release date	24/03/05	01/04/00	08/08/05	31/05/05
Latest release	26/08/05	01/04/00	29/09/06	06/06/09

[a] Started summer 2005, updated summer 2009
[b] Idea Future Public License

After the project start, Zocalo was launched in September 2005. Zocalo is a Java application designed for running prediction market experiments in classes. The first releases did not support a database backend, preventing this platform keeping a history of the transactions, nor could it run more than a one-day session. Currently, Zocalo is a unique free software platform, still in development, and includes many features such as an MSR market maker, CDA or CDAwMM book of orders.

4.8.3. Diagram of the database

The database is organized around the trader and claim tables. To meet our need for information on the users' behavior, we record all events in an *event* table. The tables *bak_** are used with a daily script to back up the data, removing confidential information, in order to be able to transmit the database for further research, guaranteeing the confidentiality and anonymity of the market. The tables are in principle managed by a class of the same name.

4.8.4. Diagram of the classes

The application, developed in Python, rests on an IF package, which includes all the principal classes of the platform. These classes are called by Python pages composing the user interface.

The classes are derived from the developments of USIFEX by Peter McCluskey. After some tedious adaptation work in order to be able to run the platform on current systems, we began to completely document all the code to mitigate the complete lack of documentation of the system. This initial adaptation and documentation work, although not very visible, currently enables us to have a transparent and comprehensible system.

After this first phase, we began to adapt the platform to our needs, regarding our design requirements. That led us to partially rewrite some classes such as IFMarketMaker, IFMarginRules and IFQuote. Furthermore, we had to change the interface and the authentication stack to suit our design requirements.

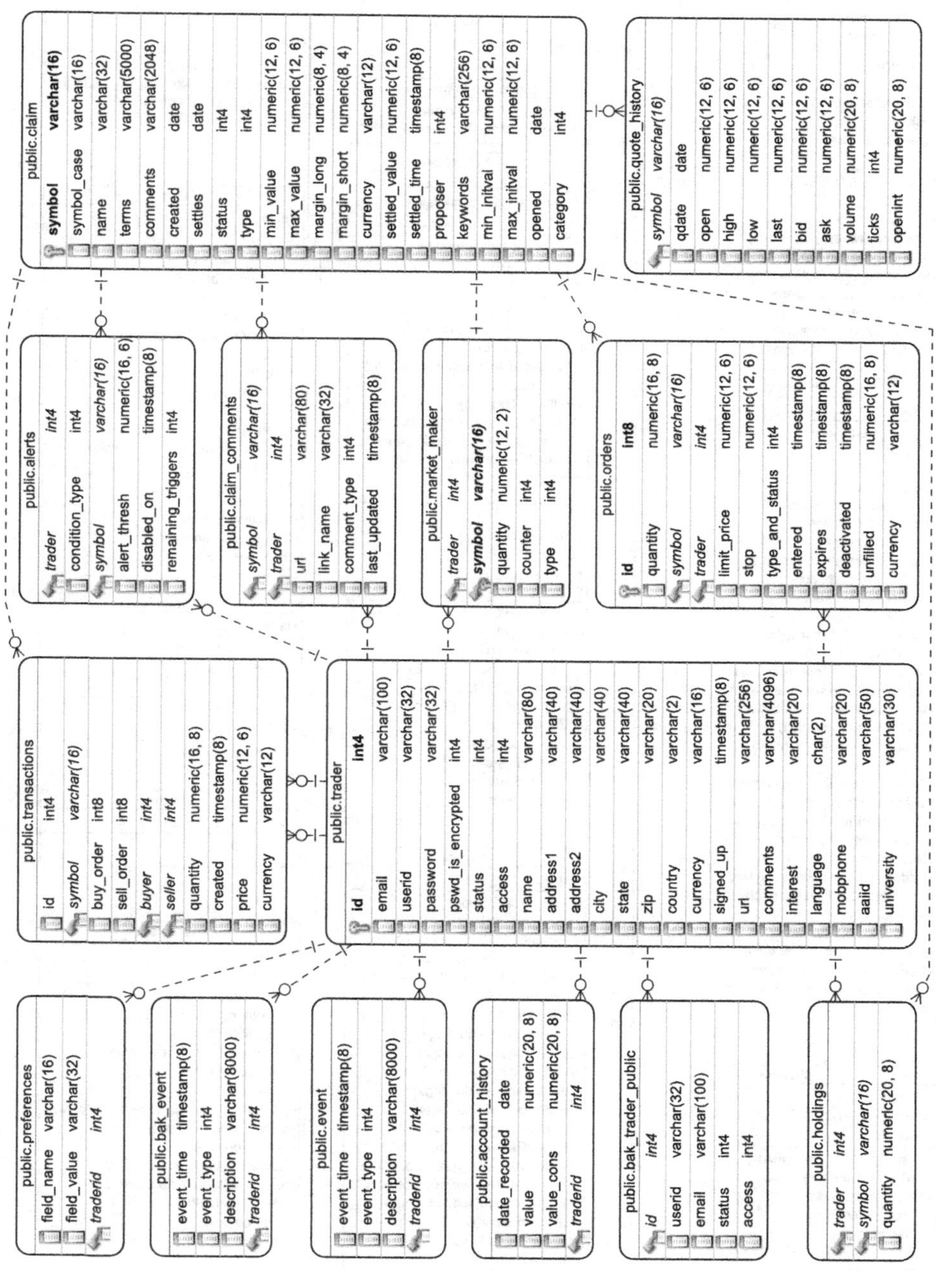

Figure 4.14.: Entity-relation diagram of the database

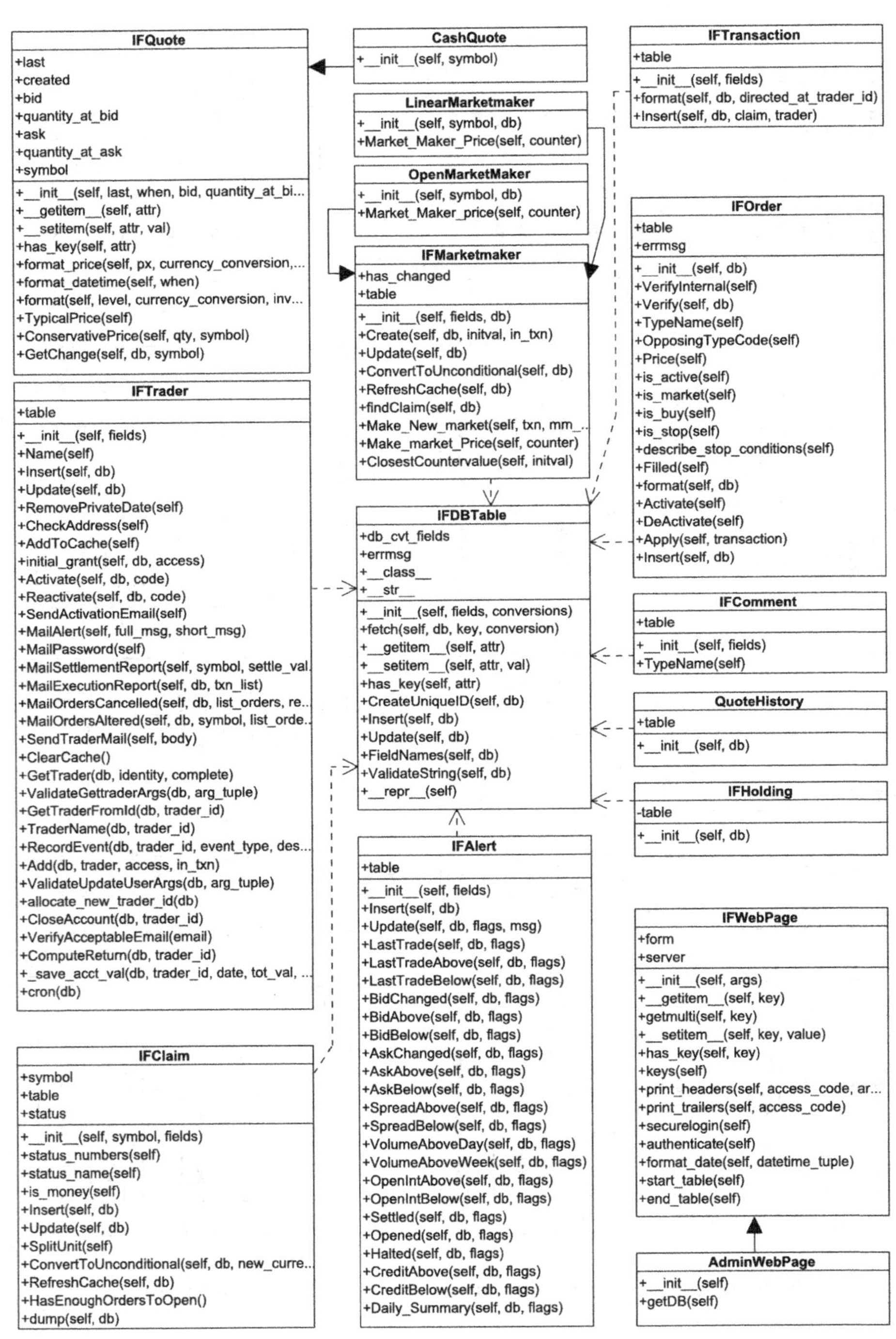

Figure 4.15.: Classes diagram of the package IF

We will now briefly present the main classes of the package IF. Other classes, in particular the classes used for the user interface, as well as more detailed information, can be retrieved from the application's current source code.

IFAlert This class handles emails sent to traders informing them of price variations concerning contracts they are subscribed to. It also generates a weekly summary of the transactions.

IFClaim Manages the claims on the market (proposal, validation, modifications and deletion).

IFComment Handles the comments and information linked to the claims. It is used mainly during the page creation.

IFHolding Manages the trader's claims portfolio. This class also supports the portfolio update after a transaction.

IFMarginRules Calculates the margin resulting from the trader's portfolio at time t. It also calculates the daily profits.

IFMarketMaker While being based on Hanson's work, this class manages an automatic market maker which guarantees enough liquidity on the market.

IFOrder This class manages buy and sale orders submitted by the traders. It is also called by the cron to process stop or LIMIT orders.

IFQuote Calculates the value of a claim at time t.

IFQuoteHistory Allows recall of the evolution of a claim's quote and can graph the result.

IFServer Handles the engine of the platform. It manages access to all the other modules and supports the principal functions (user management, claims management, portfolio management and performance calculation).

IFTrader Manages the traders (inscription, validation, modifications and deletion).

IFTransaction This class carries out the transactions between two traders (or market maker) according to the submitted orders.

4.8.5. Infrastructure

The MarMix platform was installed on a virtual host VMWare ESX 2.5 with a Debian 4 distribution. This choice was made partly because of the author's knowledge of Debian distributions as well as their relatively few attack risks due to their package's policy and to support—at any time—moving the virtual host onto another server if a power increase was needed.

For maximum security, only official Debian packages were used for the installation of the platform. The principal packages used were:

- Apache 2.0.54
- PostgreSQL 7.4.7
- Python 2.3
- PyGresql 3.6.1

Over the years, the platform has evolved to run on updated versions of the infrastructure.

4.8.6. Development

The development tools used were Eric3 (and then Eric4), a Python IDE running on Windows, OSX and GNU/Linux. It offers the advantage of having a very good debugger and of being interfaced with version control systems (CVS or SVN).

4.8.7. Prototype

The MarMix platform is based on three different pieces of software, the most important being the prediction market itself, based on IF.

We also use MediaWiki to support the documentation, the help, and the presentations and discussions of the claims. MediaWiki—the engine of Wikipedia—supports the creation and editing of content in a very intuitive way. This community-edited wiki allows each trader to add information, increase the handbook or describe its strategies. We also use the discussion tabs to keep track of the emergence of information connected with various claims. This should help us to correlate the evolution of the market price according to the emergence and the relevance of information at the disposal of the users.

Finally, we used the Shibboleth infrastructure to integer the authentication on MarMix with the Swiss Universities Authentication and Authorization Infrastructure (AAI).

For more information on the prototype, please see [50], which presents the first MarMix prototype in a very detailed way.

4.9. Contributions

4.9.1. A design artifact

We designed MarMix as a prediction market tailored to the needs of an academic research community. Our prototype could be used to support multiple experiments in various fields. Moreover, our artifact could easily be adapted to other types of outcomes due to its flexible construction. We also designed an IPO process to support the creation and proposition of new claims by the active traders, without an external review process.

In this case, our academic contribution is the generic specifications of a prediction market artifact that can be further used and developed for various prediction market applications. It follows Gregor and Jones [60] ISDT definition, "allowing the prescription of guidelines for further artifacts of the same type".

4.9.2. An exhaustive typology to support the design of a prediction market

To support our design, we developed an exhaustive typology to assist the selection of the various design factors. This complete repository of design factors and their relations could greatly improve the overall design process to run various prediction markets in different contexts. Moreover, we assume that this typology could be successfully adapted to support the generation of various configurations based on different sets of rules. Given Doty and Glick[43], a typology is an academic contribution if it is exhaustive and supports all the various representations of the studied body, which we have done in this chapter.

Part III.

Three Applications of Prediction Markets

5. Prototyping a PM for Collective Forecasting

This chapter summarizes our first iteration, studying prediction markets for collective forecasting [1]*. We build, instantiate and evaluate a prediction market in an academic context. The evaluation of these experiments led us to formulate five design propositions.*

5.1. Introduction

Currently, the main part of the literature on applications of prediction markets concentrates around three main topics: sport events, elections and the box office success of movies. These studies show that prediction markets are *a good way of incorporating information concerning the outcome of these events.* However, there are very few studies on applications in the field of science or business. We aim to determine the key success factors for the implementation of prediction markets for these new topics. Our aim is not to make an empirical validation of the results of predictions in these domains, but rather to validate the design of a prediction market adapted to this type of forecast. After describing the usage, and the context in which we will evaluate our design, we present the experiments we made and the results we obtained. Finally, we present five design propositions resulting from our design experiments.

1. The content of this chapter was partially published in [55]: C. Gaspoz and Y. Pigneur. Preparing a Negotiated R&D Portfolio with a Prediction Market, *41st Hawaii International Conference on System Science (HICSS-41)*, Hawaii, 2008.

5.2. Usage

Prediction markets have been shown to be reliable at predicting simple events in a near future as seen in section 2.8. Our goal is to explore usages of prediction markets for a new set of claims. These claims should differ from traditional political or sports claims in that they are far more complex.

Taking a political claim like "Will candidate C be elected..." is rather trivial to understand. On the other hand, "Will ultra low band (ULB) sensor networks be deployed in real life situations before..." is much harder. It supposes thorough knowledge of ULB, sensors networks and their possible usages. It also supposes knowledge of current experiments and their results, as well as the issues relating to the mass production of these devices. Given these criteria, there should be only a handful of people able to answer this question.

Prediction markets used for technological foresight should help to overcome these limitations. Due to their ability to aggregate large amounts of dispersed information in an efficient way, prediction markets should be able to answer complex questions, collecting bits of information held by a large crowd. Taking our previous example, this could be collecting information held by various stakeholders such as scholars, engineers, designers and politicians, all working on parts of the subject. The scholar could be working on ULB transmissions, the engineer on sensors networks, the designer on a sensor product and the politician on the regulation of ULB. Bringing together and efficiently aggregating this information could lead to an informed prediction.

Wolfers and Zitzewitz [172] showed that uninformed traders are necessary to bring enough liquidity to prediction markets; we make the assumption that taking a large crowd of partly informed traders could help to solve complex predictions in corporate or academic contexts.

5.3. Context

Inspired by previous experiments made with political, sports and box office prediction markets, we want to study the feasibility of implementing prediction markets for business and science forecasting.

Although innovative, these new applications of prediction markets can be based on the encouraging results of experiments made in other fields. In order to test the implementation of the design factors that we defined in chapter 4, we ran four experiments in order to test different design settings.

Our objective was to evaluate the feasibility of using prediction markets in a corporate or academic context. This comprises two parts: the aptitude of prediction markets to forecast corporate or academic claims and the adequacy of the tool for the corporate or academic environment.

5.3.1. Aptitude

Prediction markets have shown that they are reliable at predicting sports or political events. These events are characterized by the fact that they are very easy to understand (candidate *X* will be elected or team *Y* will win the match) and are the subject of a mass of publicly available information.

On the other hand, business or R&D events (how many sales of product *X* will be made during time *T* or which R&D project has the greatest potential on the market) are much more difficult to define and are the subject to little or no publicly available information.

Our experiments must show whether if it is possible to apply a prediction method that was designed for relatively basic claims to complex ones and whether the aggregation and information retrieval mechanisms are powerful enough to collect sufficient information to obtain significant predictions.

Table 5.1.: Prediction markets claims

	Political or sport PM	Corporate or academic PM
Type of claims	Basic	Complex
Information characteristics	Abundant and public	Limited and private

5.3.2. Adequacy

Although recent studies, as we saw in section 2.5, show that the motivation of the traders on political prediction markets is sufficient to obtain reliable results, it is not yet proven whether the motivation of corporate or academic players is sufficient to obtain significant results too.

On public prediction markets, traders play in the hope of future profits that could take a pecuniary form, the form of prizes or simply the form of recognition by their peers. In addition, the information that they have has, in general, little or no value for the trader. The potential profits on the market generally represent the best profits that they could expect from this information.

On the other hand, the applications we plan to study will be addressed to people who have a well-defined activity and who will be asked to invest time on an extra activity. Moreover, they will mostly not directly benefit from the outcomes of the market for their professional activities, apart from the few people who could benefit from the results of the markets. In addition, the value of information held by traders is definitely higher in this context. This value can be pecuniary, but also personal, for example, for a future promotion. So the motivation process of the players must be much more advanced than in public markets.

Our experiments must show which requirements are necessary so that employees and researchers invest time on prediction markets and share sufficient and qualitatively good information to reach a significant equilibrium price.

Table 5.2.: Prediction markets incentives

	Political or sport PM	Corporate or academic PM
Incentive to play	Direct profit (money, prize)	Indirect profit
Incentive to reveal	Strong	Weak

5.4. Evaluation > Four design experiments

We chose to follow Hevner et al. [84] design science methodology in an iterative process of building and evaluating artifacts. With this intention, we successively created and operated four prediction markets with different populations (see Table 5.3). The contracts were related to economic, scientific and political forecasts, as well as to sport events. These four iterations enabled us to evaluate our design, adapt it, and implement it in a new experiment. This chapter presents the four iterations and describes the resulting five design proposals.

5.4.1. An experimental prototype

We started our first iteration with the design of an experimental prototype for a small number of traders. This first prototype was used for an experiment within the Information Systems Institute of the University of Lausanne. The main goal of this experiment was to test our design in a real-life environment and to explore the incentive mechanisms.

Experimenting with a simple prediction market

This first iteration began with the design of a prediction market, based on the design constraints addressed in chapter 4. We then operated the prediction market and conducted several exploratory interviews with the actors having participated in the experiment at the end of October 2005.

Table 5.3.: Presentation of the four prediction markets

Prediction Market	Description
MarMix(I)	**Experimental prototype** – Run with 28 traders among the Information Systems Institute staff at HEC Lausanne. Contracts on votations, science findings and mobile information technologies.
MarMix(II)	**Large-scale market** – Run with 114 undergraduate students in business and economics at HEC Lausanne. Contracts on financial indices, mobile information technologies, general science challenges as well as FIFA World Cup matches.
2014candidates.org	**Topic-focused market** – Run with 52 traders among national and international sport federations as well as sports consultants. This market was designed to predict the organizing city of the 2014 Winter Olympic Games.
MarMICS	**Technological foresight market** – Run with 150 PhD students working for the Swiss National Science Foundation (SNSF) project MICS (Mobile Information and Communication Systems). Contracts on MICS projects outcomes.

The intention of this first experiment was above all to test our prediction market in a *real-life context*. This experiment gave us the opportunity to test the various components of the prediction market. It also enabled us to implement and test the design choices elaborated during the previous design phase (chapter 4).

We tested a simple prediction market with a small number of actors, given that researchers such as Chen et al. [28] or Christiansen [33] found that small markets are also able to make accurate predictions. This configuration gave us the ability to run the test with well-known participants. Furthermore, due the few traders involved, we had the ability to get feedback from all participants during the experiment.

First implementation of the design

The main design options resulting from the interviews carried with the MICS project leaders and other associated researchers were implemented in this prototype.

Confidentiality The main fear regarding the use of a prediction market in a research community is the confidentiality of both the claims and the predictions. For the project leaders, the willingness to participate and share information on such a platform is dependent on the guarantee of this confidentiality. The feeling in the academic community is that only published ideas have real value. Given that, sharing research intuition on a market could be potentially risky for researchers. Therefore we decided to only trade on claims relating to published papers. Furthermore the disclosure of predictions regarding running projects could have a negative (or positive) impact on the allowance of research subsidies from the sponsors. To assess this issue, we linked our prediction market to the authorisation infrastructure of the swiss universities.

Anonymity In the same vein, the market has to guarantee the anonymity of all traders and transactions. This is related to the eventuality of hierarchical and group pressures on the traders. Solving this issue is very easy, and we chose to use nicknames freely chosen by the traders. At the first login, traders are asked to choose a nickname and are informed of its use on the platform.

Attractivity In a research community, the ideation process is very important. To support it, the market should be able to attract these new research intuitions. The goal of such a market being to suppress the established peer review process, we chose to implement an initial public offering (IPO) process, allowing each participant to submit new claims on the market.

Liquidity As previously discussed in section 2.7 the market operator has to guarantee enough liquidity to improve the accuracy of the prediction market. Furthermore, traders should be able to make transactions independently from other traders' counter orders. From the different options, we chose to implement a simple continuous double auction mechanism with a market maker (CDAwMM). The market maker orders are illustrated by the suffix *mm* coupled with the claim name (Figure 5.1).

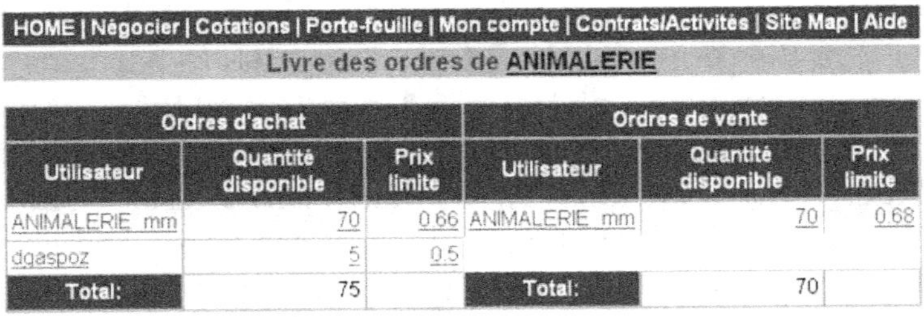

HOME | Négocier | Cotations | Porte-feuille | Mon compte | Contrats/Activités | Site Map | Aide

Livre des ordres de ANIMALERIE

Ordres d'achat			Ordres de vente		
Utilisateur	Quantité disponible	Prix limite	Utilisateur	Quantité disponible	Prix limite
ANIMALERIE_mm	70	0.66	ANIMALERIE_mm	70	0.68
dgaspoz	5	0.5			
Total:	75		Total:	70	

Figure 5.1.: The order book of the ANIMALERIE claim with the market maker positions

Adding the design choices previously described to the main options retained in chapter 4, we obtain the specifications for our first prototype as stated in Table 5.4.1. These specifications were already presented in section 4.8 and are repeated here to simplify the reading.

Table 5.4.: Design specifications of the first prototype

Incentive mechanisms	Performance	Performance evaluation	Wealth: portfolio-value based
		Performance measurement	Last trading price
	Reward	Reward type	Non-monetary (prize)
		Reward base	Tournament: performance-based
	Involvement		Trading sessions
Trading process	Fees		No fees
	Trading mechanisms	Double auction	Open order book
		Market maker	CDAwMM
	Trading time		24/7
Investor management	Market	Market policy	Closed market
		Market transparency	Display all information
	Investor	Investor anonymity	Username
		Investor unicity	Enforced (Switch AAI)[a]
		Investor selection	All project members

[a] Swiss Universities Authentication and Authorization Infrastructure

Table 5.5.: Design specifications of the first prototype (continued)

Clearing house	Order	Order matching rules	Price and submission
		Order spending caps	No caps
		Order type	Market and limit
		Short selling	Allowed
	Asset	Asset type	Play-money
		Inflation	No
		Borrowing	Yes
		Endowment	Initial endowment: Play-money
	Claim	Claim IPO	Fees and rewards: No Screening: Only for the wording
		Initial claims	Starting quotes: IPO Quantity: 5
		Claim ontology	Enforced for claim's proposals
		Claim type	Winner-take-all[b]
		Claim structure	Independent
	Payoff	Settlement date	Public
		Settlement judge	Claim's owner
		Settlement price	Final market price

[b] Also called Arrow-Debreu

Operating the prediction market

We used the prediction market for a one-hour laboratory experiment with 15 researchers trading five binary contracts (Table 5.6), followed by a two-week experiment during which about 30 traders (including the first 15) were able to trade the same five contracts. The contracts were not specifically designed for technological forecasting, but were selected for their estimated capacity to motivate the players to take part in the experiment. Given our main research goal, we voluntarily neglected contracts on sport events or elections.

Table 5.6.: Claims used for the first iteration

ANIMALERIE	Result of the vote on the construction of a breeding farm for the university
MOB	First-large scale mobile payment experiment in Switzerland in 2006
MSCBIS	More than 15 masters students registered for the new MScBIS
SENSOR	Large-scale sensor network to predict the risks of avalanche in the swiss alps
WEATHER	Rain in Lausanne on November 11

The prediction market was available through a web browser from anywhere. This allowed traders to play as they like. Its interface (Figure 5.2) was strongly inspired by traditional stock markets, with multiple options like *selling short, limit orders* and *market orders*. As we will see later, this gave us great flexibility, sometimes to the detriment of the traders.

First observations from our implementation

To evaluate our design, we conducted several exploratory interviews with the traders who participated in the experiment at the end of October 2005.

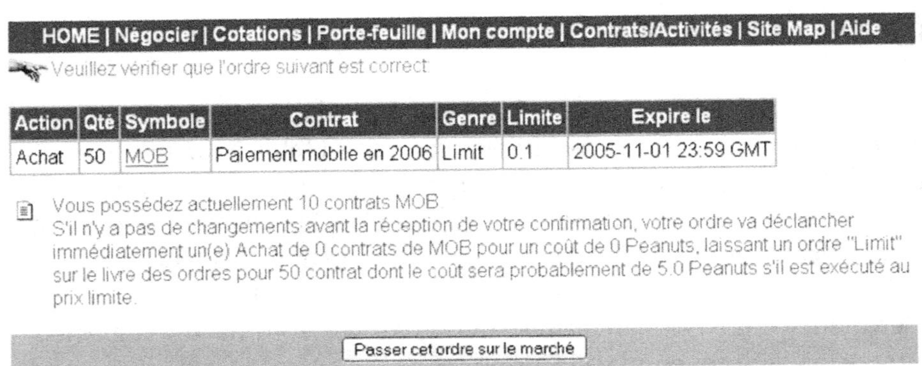

Figure 5.2.: The user interface of the first prototype

During this first experiment we collected various pieces of information about the use of the market by the traders. These data enabled us to determine the participation rate of the users, the movements on the various claims as well as the return rate of the users, as seen in Table 5.7. After analyzing the data we note that there are very few users who played regularly apart from the one-hour workshop and almost no users played during the two weeks if they had not taken part in the workshop. At the contract level we see that most of the transactions were carried out during the workshop, although we also see a peak of activity before the expiration of the *ANIMALERIE* claim, which was linked to the results of a vote on the construction of a new breeding farm for the university.

Table 5.7.: Key numbers resulting from the first experiment

Number of traders	28
Number of active traders (> 3 orders)	11
Average orders by trader	26
Number of claims	5
Number of orders	286
Number of contracts	5093

The considerable variation in the participants' involvement between the two parts of the experiment (synchronous and asynchronous trading) showed us that the basic mechanisms of futures markets were not known by the IS researchers and that, consequently, without direct supervision and a well-defined incentive mechanism, IS researchers were not motivated to trade on such a market.

This analysis helped us to illustrate the use of a prediction market in a concrete and observable setting. However, it had several limitations that prevented us from obtaining a deeper understanding of the problem.

Cultural shift The first observation resulting from the interviews was that the researchers are by no means familiar with the concepts necessary for playing on a prediction market. The underlying concepts such as limit orders, selling short and compensation of the portfolios are not mastered by the traders, which results in errors or discourages them from playing on the market.

Interface design The second observation is related to the interface. The study of the use cases led us to develop a multi-part prototype so as to cover the various functions. This resulted in a highly partitioned interface, presenting each function independently. This disturbed the traders, who did not find the necessary information to take the right decision of investment and who did not have the overall picture of their individual performances on the various titles, nor a comparison with the other traders.

Based on these considerations, we revised our design and developed a second prototype. In the following subsection we show the results of a highly improved prediction market that will give us more insights.

5.4.2. Improving interaction for a large-scale experiment

After our first small-scale experiment, we decided to run a second large-scale experiment to test the design of the prototype. This second experiment took place at the Business School of the University of Lausanne with 114 traders, playing during six weeks on 16 claims in summer 2006. During the whole experiment, we had a total of 3071 transactions, representing 144248 contracts.

An improved human–computer interface

Based on the results of the first experiment, we decided to completely rewrite the user interface to improve the user experience. Our goal was to develop a very intuitive interface in terms of usability, hiding the excessively financial aspects of the marketplace, in order to reduce the learning curve, as illustrated in Figure 5.3.

An open-source application framework

This second iteration gave us the opportunity to improve the design of the market's functionalities. Based on the four use cases presented in section 4.5, we improved the interactions between the market and the traders.

Development of the trader's cockpit In order to play on the market, the trader needs enough private information to optimize his return on investment, and also enough information from the market to take the right investment decision. For this purpose, we provided a range of decision support information such as graphics with daily, weekly, monthly and complete quote histories, historics of the daily quotes with trends and summaries, various top ten lists such as the biggest movements, gains, losses and the most active traders and claims. We also extended the real-time quotes with short- and long-term trends for each claim. Most of

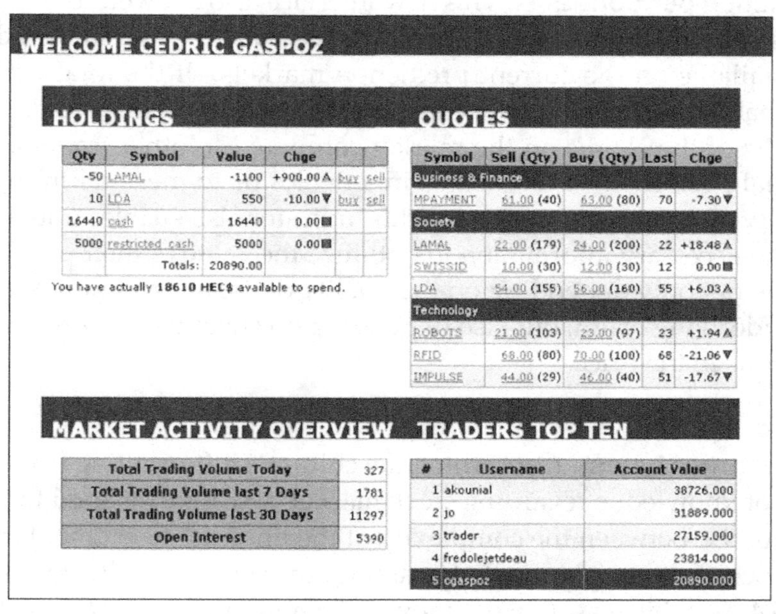

Figure 5.3.: The MarMix prediction market with a new user interface

this information is included on the new trader's cockpit (Figure 5.3). This personal cockpit summarizes in one place all the important information needed to play on the market, e.g. actual quotes, individual performance on each claim, most active claims, daily, weekly and monthly exchange volume and the overall performance of the trader. The last indicator is used to reward the best players at the end of the experiment.

Performance per contract This new interface also allowed us to introduce the concept of performance per contract, which, to our knowledge, is not available on the current prediction markets. If the total performance enables us to obtain information on our global capacity to predict the results of the claims on the market compared to other traders, the individual performance on each claim enables us to measure in detail the quality of each of our forecasts. This indicator also enables traders to obtain the necessary information to optimize the value of their portfolio, this value not only depending on the quality of the information related to the underlying claim, but also depending on short-term profit-based fluctuations in the price.

Reduced order types Concerning the cultural shift resulting from the absence of knowledge regarding stock market concepts, we tried to find a compromise between the complexity of the financial instruments and the absence of financial knowledge among the traders, as illustrated in Figure 5.4. For this reason, we removed the notion of *stop orders* on this new interface, to keep only *market* and *limit orders*. These two order types are mandatory to use both double auction and automated market maker ways of placing orders in our CDAwMM implementation.

One-click trading We also added a *one-click trading* option to allow traders to pass market orders by directly clicking on a quote or to pass limit orders by clicking on the reverse transaction on order books.

Finally, we tried to remove as far as possible financial terms from the interface. It was not possible to do this altogether and we had to maintain

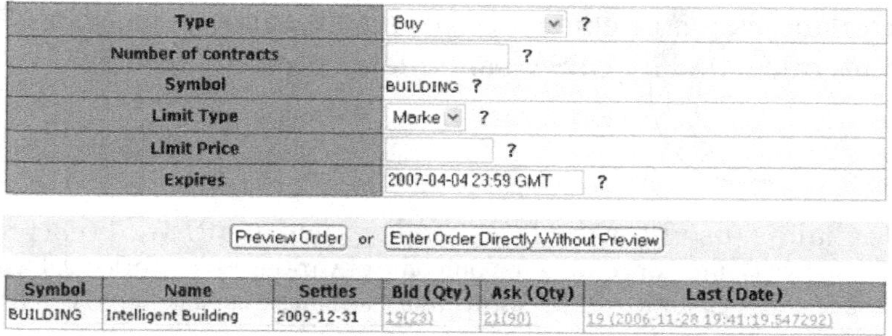

Figure 5.4.: The order screen of MarMix

some financial concepts, such as the notion of limit orders.

A large-scale experiment

To evaluate our second design, we operated a large-scale prediction market with 99 active traders, most of whom were students in economics at the University of Lausanne. For this experiment, we decided to choose more generic claims, based on finance, society, technology and sport (FIFA World Cup).

Table 5.8.: Key numbers resulting from the second experiment

Number of traders	114
Number of active traders (> 3 orders)	99
Average orders by trader	31
Number of claims	16
Number of orders	3071
Number of contracts	144248

Among the 16 claims (Table 5.9), the market correctly predicted the outcome of eight. Seven were not settled at the end of the experiment and the last claim missed the prediction. This claim was a sports claim relying on the rank of Switzerland at the FIFA World Cup, predicting that Switzerland would be eliminated during the quarter-finals, based on probabilities calculated by UBS Wealth Management Research.

Table 5.9.: Claims' used for the large-scale experiment. We do not present the five claims concerning the outcome of various FIFA World CUP games. Each FIFA claim was in the form: *Team A will win the game Team A vs Team B.*

ITALIE	Italy to be World Champions 06
SUISSE	Switzerland eliminated in quarter-final
IMPULSE	SolarImpulse first night flight in 2009
ALINGHI	Alinghi wins America's Cup 07
LDA	Law on royalties voted in by parliament
MOBILE	First large-scale mobile payment experiment in Switzerland in 2006
SWISSID	Numerical identity provided on Swiss ID cards in 2009
VISTA	Windows VISTA released at the end of 2006
STARACH	Switzerland be part of the 6th StarAc
SMI-06	SMI exceeds 7800 in June
SMI-07	SMI exceeds 7800 in July

This large-scale experiment gave us the opportunity to see how the market reacted to the information. As stated in many papers, prediction markets should quickly react to new information. We did indeed observe this rapid reaction for many claims. The easiest way to notice it is by comparing the quotes of the SMI-07 claim on MarMix with the quotes of the Swiss Market Index (SMI). The SMI-07 claim was opened June and settled on 31 July. In Figure 5.5, we can see both quotes and how the SMI-07 curve slightly anticipated the variations of the SMI. Around 15 July, we note that the prediction market anticipated the rate's recovery two days in advance.

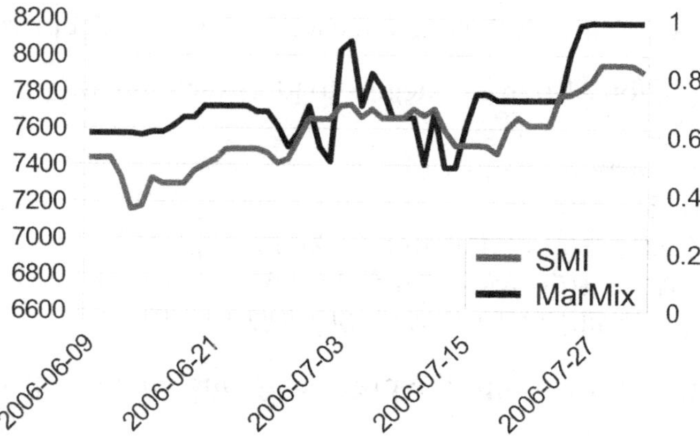

Figure 5.5.: Variation of the Swiss Market Index and the SMI-07 claim on MarMix

Improved user experience

In comparison with the first design, we noticed that 89% of the registered traders were active during the six weeks. This result confirms that a better user interface was crucial. With a ten-minute presentation, most of the traders understood the principles and how to play on the market. We also tried to communicate the information to the traders via many different channels such as email and information displays at the university. The latter played an important role in motivating the traders, and in some cases was more important than the prize itself.

Market maker failure We rapidly realized that the chosen automated market maker algorithm, was not designed to support large-scale experiments. The market price over-reacted if many small orders and, in particular, short orders were put in, allowing traders to make disproportionate profits. Although this algorithm worked well on a small market, the number of concurrent orders placed on this large market showed the limits of our choice. Entering 20 buy or sell orders was enough to change the market price by up to 40%. Moreover, this function did not take into account the open orders in the book to establish the market price.

- Choose a function $M(i)$ from integers to $[0, 1]$ such that $M(i) > M(i + 1)$ and $M(0) = 1/2$
- Choose a transaction quantity Q
- Market starts at $j = 0$
- Offer "\$Q if A" $\rightarrow$ \$$(Q * M(j))$ and if taken $j \rightarrow j + 1$
- Offer "\$Q if A" $\leftarrow$ \$$(Q * M(j + 1))$ and if taken $j \rightarrow j - 1$
- If $M(i) = 1/(1 + exp(i/k))$, total loss $\lesssim \$Q * k/2$

For this experiment, we kept the previously implemented price function.

$$P(x) = min_{value} + (max_{value} - min_{value}) * 1.0/(1.0 + exp(0.1 * j))$$

After reviewing the literature we chose the design proposition of Robin Hanson based both on a combinatorial market maker algorithm and on a book of orders [71]. This proposition is based on two other publications by Hanson, the Logarithmic Market Scoring Rules [80] and the Combinatorial Information Market Design [75]. This implementation is currently used in many prediction markets, including Zocalo[2]. Recently Berg and Proebsting [12] presented their implementation of Hanson's automated market maker with a complete mathematical model.

Finally, this second experiment gave us the opportunity to test our prototype over a long period of time, with a large market and a huge number of transactions. Except for the market-maker algorithm problem, we consider this second prototype robust enough to run more experiments.

5.4.3. Redeploying the market for policy analysis

In collaboration with the Swiss Graduate School of Public Administration, we ran an experiment based on the same prototype, dedicated to the prediction of the organizing city of the 2014 Winter Olympic Games,

2. Zocalo is a free java prediction market software available at `http://zocalo.sf.net`

with 52 traders coming from various international and national sport federations and specialized media.

A highly sensitive topic

Due to the sensitiveness of the topic for our partner, we set up an *invitation only* prediction market with national and international key players. They were invited to play on seven claims concerning the selection of the candidates' cities for the organization of the 2014 Winter Olympic Games (Figure 5.6). The aim of the market was to predict the two to four cities retained on the short list during the June 22, 2006 IOC meeting.

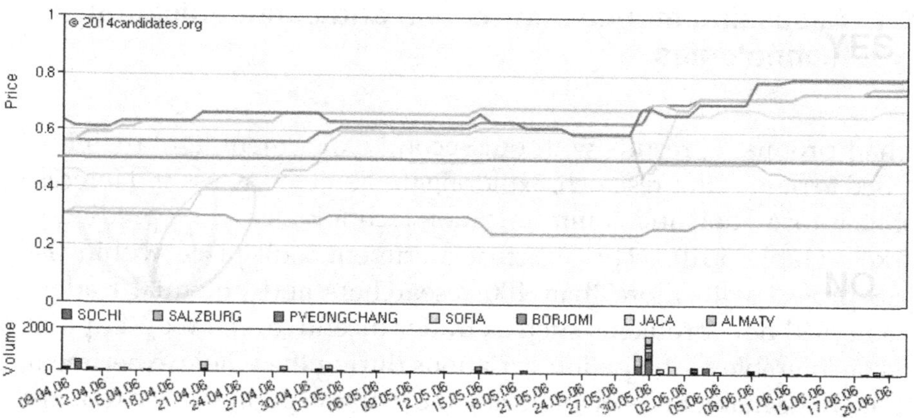

Figure 5.6.: 2014candidates.org – Claim quotes during the experiment

An aborted initiative

During the experiment, our partner had to leave the project for political reasons and we decided to let the market run till June 22, but to stop the experiment at that point. We did however, notice that the market found the three nominated cities but overevalued the chances of Sofia, which settled with a price over 50%.

In conclusion, we started this project based on numerous contributions on prediction market applications for public policy and decision making [44, 67, 100], which show that prediction markets could sucessfully be used to solve these problems. However, we encountered totally new issues, namely that the policy makers were not disposed to publicly inform on these topics. Until now, the unique case concerning a failure in the implementation of a prediction market for public policy was the Policy Analysis Market (PAM) developed by Hanson [79, 137]. Hovewer, we now know that the main consideration in aborting the project was not directly a problem with the project itself [77].

5.4.4. Assessing mobile information and communication technologies

We had promising results with our second experiment, and therefore decided to pursue this research, exploring the ability to assess and forecast mobile information and communication technologies using prediction markets (Table 5.10). This fourth experiment took place within the MICS project with more than 100 researchers and potential traders. We assessed new problems such as trader incentive, claim description and considerable participation variations during the whole experiment. Although the market was open during the whole experiment, we thought of having participation peaks during the bi-annual project events.

Improved design

We improved our second prototype slightly for this fourth experiment, based on a better automated market maker and a more adapted ontology for technological claims. Moreover, we included the possibility of playing by mobile phone, allowing us to run experiments during workshops and conferences.

Table 5.10.: Claims list at the beginning of the third iteration

CAR	Large-scale (10 vehicles) vehicular network test
AVALANCHE	Sensor-networks deployed by the Swiss Federal Institute for Snow and Avalanche to detect the risks of avalanche in Alpine regions
RFID	Mobile phones with RFID in Switzerland
ROBOTS	Robots detect a ringing phone among a hundred faster than humans
MPAYMENT	At MICS meeting of 2009, the majority of the participants will pay for their train ticket by mobile phone
BUILDING	Users helped by ludic interfaces are better than intelligent buildings in energy saving

Ontology for technological claims To asses more complex topics such as technological claims, we developed a sort of specific ontology to describe technological claims. The goal of this ontology is to standardize the description of the claims so as to allow researchers coming from other fields to quickly understand the underlying concepts. Our ontology takes the concepts of the futures markets and adds the specific concepts of the description of scientific research. A more detailled presentation of this ontology follows in section 5.5.1.

Ubiquitous access For the last iteration we added the possibility to trade via cellular phones, based on the short text messages (SMS) exchange. In addition to the advantages in terms of portability, this development allowed us to simplify the interactions between the traders and the platform. We developed a language syntax to reduce the instructions to the minimum, and to ensure that the exchanged messages conform to the SMS format, as presented in Table 5.11. This enables the user to send, for example, *MARMIX BUY 25 SENSOR* to pass an order for 25 contracts of the claim sensor at the market price on the MarMix prediction market.

Table 5.11.: Example of text messages used to trade by cellular phone on MarMix

BUY	To buy a certain number of contracts at the market price or to place a limit order For example: *MICS BUY 23 RFID* [*LIMIT 0.67*]
QUOTE	To get a particular quote or all the active claim quotes For example: *MICS QUOTE RFID* or *MICS QUOTE LIST*
HOLDINGS	To get an overview of the portfolio For example: *MICS HOLDINGS*
ORDERS	To manage open orders (delete or change the limit price or the quantity) For example: *MICS ORDERS DELETE 78787*

Finally, to assure the confidentiality of the market, we completely anonymized the platform, and also restricted access to only members of the project community.

First experiment with researchers

To ensure that the study was relevant, we started the market during an MICS workshop in the presence of 100 researchers. We proceeded in the same way as for the initial prototype (section 5.4.1) with a workshop in the presence of computer scientists and telecoms engineers without any financial background, followed by a long-term experiment. However, we did not have permanent direct access to the whole research community and hence had only a few active traders (Figure 5.7).

We tried different strategies for motivating the scientists to trade on the prediction market such as presentations and demos at workshops, monthly information in the project newsletter and direct contacts when available. After a first series of interviews we noticed that was a reasonable level of interest within the community for this type of technology but that the teams were centered on specific problems, and it was difficult to

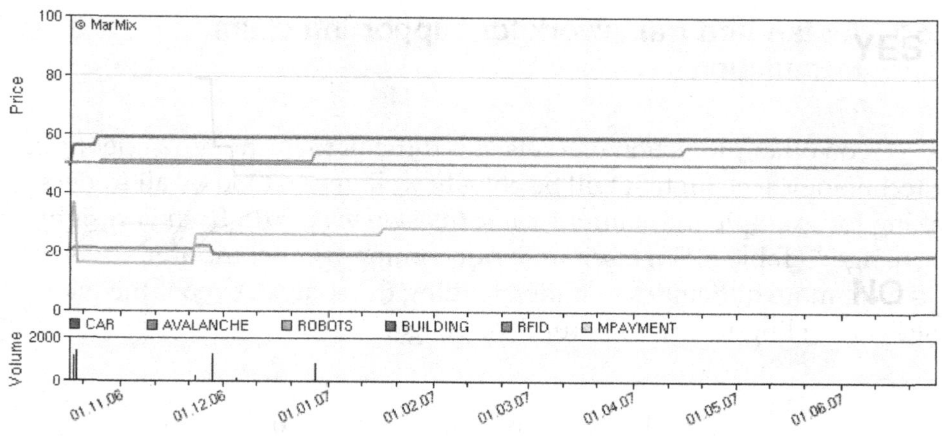

Figure 5.7.: MICS — Claim quotes during the experiment

get them interested in questions outside their field of work.

This experiment gave us the incentive to redesign our platform and to further develop our knowledge of running prediction markets in different contexts. We aborted the experiment at the end of 2008, with a new understanding of the incentive mechanisms.

5.5. Findings from four experiments

Following a design science methodology as stated in section 5.1, we ran four different implementations of our prediction market. Each implementation was the occasion to improve and test our design. From the evaluation of these design–evaluate loops, we noticed five relevant issues related to our design choices as well as our test environment: *the description of the claims* (sections 5.4.1 and 5.4.4), *the IPO process* (5.4.1 and 5.4.4), *the abstraction of the financial concepts* (5.4.1, 5.4.2, 5.4.3 and 5.4.4), *the support of synchronous and asynchronous trading* (5.4.1 and 5.4.4) and *the presence of a market maker* (5.4.1, 5.4.2, 5.4.3 and 5.4.4).

5.5.1. A standard framework for supporting claim formulation

As seen on other prediction markets, it is difficult to formulate a scientific or technological claim that will be equally well understood by all traders. Taking for example the claim *Machine translation by 2015* from Foresight Exchange[3] (Table 5.12), a scientist not coming from computer science, will have more difficulties in understanding the context, even if the main issues are in linguistic and natural language.

Table 5.12.: Machine translation by 2015

Category	Science and technology
Owner	Mats
Judge	Loophole
Created	1995/01/26
Due date	2017/12/31
The claim	By the end of the year 2015, there will be a program that can translate written material into English from one of French, German, Russian, Japanese or Chinese. The program will work well on ordinary non-fiction prose, newspaper and magazine articles, ordinary non-legalese business letters and scientific and technical writing. The translations will be of comparable cost and turnaround time, and equal or better then average quality, as professional human translations. Source text may be entered in any convenient way – this isn't an OCR claim
Judge's statement	I will judge based on the wording of the claim unless it is found to be ambiguous. Such ambiguities will be resolved based on my perception of the author's intent. I interpret "Comparable cost and turnaround time" to mean equal or lower cost and turnaround time compared to typical human translation services

3. `http://www.ideosphere.com/fx-bin/Claim?claim=Tran`

As main goal of a technological prediction market is to assess current and new technologies, it is of great importance that all traders get the same comprehension of the underlying issues. We propose a claim ontology to support the formulation of technological claims.

The goal of this ontology is to standardize the description of the claims to allow traders coming from other domains to quickly understand the underlying concepts. Our ontology takes the concepts of the futures markets and adds the specific concepts of the description of R&D projects. Currently, the focus of the presented ontology is on research projects rather than on development ones.

To our knowledge, there is currently no ontology applicable to prediction market claims. The closest ontology could be in the financial fields or in the commodities futures. The design of a clean ontology exceeds the framework of this work and could be the subject of future research on prediction markets.

Initially, we studied the correspondence with the commodities futures, which are closely linked to prediction markets. Take, for example, a future on cocoa traded on the New York Board of Trade (Table 5.13).

Most information is related to the terms of the agreement: symbol, name, market, unit, market's opening and value of the contracts. One will note the description of the due dates, which are coded by letters and are associated with one day of settlement. Thus the contract CCZ5 is a cocoa contract that will expire on 15 December 2009.

This information is directly applicable to the prediction markets and can be used to describe the structure of the claims. However, as the commodity markets could not be the subject of controversy, the description of the commodities is defined in external standards.

Table 5.13.: CCZ5 cocoa future traded on the New York Board of Trade

Symbol	CC
Name	Cocoa
Exchange	NYBOT
Trading months	H,K,N,U,Z
Trading unit	10 metric tons (22,046 lbs)
Tick size	$1.00 per metric ton ($10.00 per contract)
Daily limit	None
Trading hours	8:00a.m. to 11:50a.m. EST
Last trading day	Eleven business days prior to last business day of delivery month
Value of one futures unit	$10
Value of one options unit	$10
Delivery/settlement terms	
Grade/standards/quality	Established by Exchange licensed graders in accordance with specified tolerances for defects, bean count, bean size and other standards
Deliverable growths	The growth of any country or clime, including new or yet unknown growths. Growths are divided into three classifications: Group A, deliverable at a premium of $160/ton (including the main crops of Ghana, Nigeria, Ivory Coast, among others); Group B, deliverable at a premium of $80.00/ton (includes Bahia, Arriba, Venezuela, among others); Group C, deliverable at par (includes Sanchez, Haiti, Malaysia and all others).
Delivery points	At licensed warehouses in the Port of New York District, Delaware River Port District or Port of Hampton Roads

International Cocoa Standards
The International Cocoa Standards require cocoa of merchantable quality to be fermented, thoroughly dry, free from smoky beans, free from abnormal or foreign odours and free from any evidence of adulteration. It must be reasonably free from living insects, broken beans, fragments and pieces of shell and foreign matter and reasonably uniform in size.
Throughout the world the standards against which all cocoa is measured are those of Ghana cocoa. Cocoa is graded on the basis of the count of defective beans in the cut test. Defective beans should not exceed the following limits:
Grade I
- Mouldy beans, maximum 3% by count;
- Slaty beans, maximum 3% by count;
- Insect-damaged, germinated or flat beans, total maximum 3% by count.

Grade II
- Mouldy beans, maximum 4% by count;
- Slaty beans, maximum 8% by count;
- Insect-damaged, germinated or flat beans, total maximum 6% by count.

Furthermore, we also studied the composition of prospectuses on financial markets, which are also rather close to the creation of claims on a prediction market. We based ourselves on the Commission Regulation (EC) No 809/2004 issued by the European Union concerning information contained in prospectuses.

Commission Regulation (EC) No 809/2004

A. Identity of directors, senior management, advisers and auditors

B. Offer statistics and expected timetable

C. Key information concerning selected financial data; capitalisation and indebtedness; reasons for the offer and use of proceeds; risk factors

D. Information concerning the issuer
- history and development of the issuer
- business overview

E. Operating and financial review and prospects
- research and development, patents and licences, etc.
- trends

F. Directors, senior management and employees

G. Major shareholders and related-party transactions

H. Financial information
- consolidated statement and other financial information
- significant changes

I. Details of the offer and admission to trading
- offer and admission to trading
- plan for distribution
- markets
- selling shareholders
- dilution (equity securities only)
- expenses of the issue

J. Additional information
- share capital
- memorandum and articles of association
- documents on display

In this directive, points B and I can be connected to the previous cocoa example. We also find a part that describes the details of the offer, namely the assets of the firm, its evolution, its activities. Unfortunately, the most specific part does not help us to draw a parallel with prediction market claims.

We decided to split the definition of the claims into two parts. The first relates to the elements described as structural, which define the claim's terms, and the second defines the claim's proposal.

Structural elements

The structural elements are defined in such a way that all traders are rapidly able to understand the main properties of the contract. We can define these in a formal way and use a proper ontology to describe, for example, the manner of calculating the settle value of the contract and the terms of payment. The structural elements consist of the description, the judgment, the price and the type of the claim.

The description contains the symbol, the name, the underlying project, the author and the type of contract (binary, index, …).

The judgment section describes the settle time, the manner it will be judged and by whom, and the trusted information sources for the judgment. It is also necessary to specify the applicable rules if there is no possibility of judging the claim or if the judgment cannot be settled. For example, if there is a claim about the discovery of the Higgs particle by CERN or Fermilab[4], it is necessary to specify the value of the contract if a third laboratory discovers the particle first. This particular claim states that the value of the contract will be $50 if neither of the two laboratories discovers the particle.

The price section describes the price range in which the contract will evolve, as well as the method of calculating the price at the settle time. Claims could be of the type *binary*, but could also be indexes, logarithmic functions or winner-takes-all in the case of multiple outcomes. The date of payment should also be specified if it does not take place directly after the judgment.

4. `http://news.us.newsfutures.com/market/market.html?symbol=HIGGCERN`

Claim proposal

Due to the diversity of the prediction markets and the related claims, it is difficult to propose a generic framework for defining a claim's proposal. We tried to characterize MICS claims based on the interviews carried out at the beginning of the project as well as on the active claims on the other markets. We noticed five important concepts: the sphere of activity, the state of the art, the goal of the research, the expected results and the measure of success, illustrated by the SLF claim in Table 5.14.

The state-of-the-art section gives a short presentation of the research history. In this category we describe the previous steps necessary to formulate the goal of the research, detail the related work and present some major publications in the field. Such information will enable each researcher to situate the claim in its field of research.

The goal of the research describes the expected outcome of the research after a given time. These are global, long-term and not precisely defined goals, as they represent research in progress.

The expected results are the concrete elements, in the mid term, that will result from the research. They may be products, demonstrations, patents, algorithms, creation of start-ups, standards or RFCs.

The measure of success must precisely express the methods of evaluation of the awaited results. This evaluation should be objective and factual. We could, for example, specify the product's market share, the acceptance of a demonstration by the scientific community, the use of a patent and the publication of the results by the press.

5.5.2. An easy IPO mechanism to support the innovation process

We propose to deal with the claims management in a different way from other prediction markets, which use a top-down process. Indeed, to guarantee the transmission of information between the researchers and the market, each trader should be allowed to trade on the available claims

Table 5.14.: The SLF claim on MarMix

Symbol	SLF
Name	Sensor-Network deployed by SLF
Type	Binary
Project	Real-time avalanche and landslide analysis through sensor networks
Settle date	31.07.2009
Jury	Made up of two members of the SLF, two members of the project and one person in charge of MICS
Source	SLF report the tests carried out. If there is no report, raw data of the SLF can be used
Price	Minimum price: 0, maximum: 100
Payment	Winner-takes-all (if the contract is TRUE: 1, if not: 0)
Field of research	Research on sensor-networks
State of the art	The fluid-dynamics models used so far in predicting mass movements such as avalanches rely on speculative equations and very little is known about the internal structure of avalanches. Field measurements only provide insight into shape characteristics (e.g., avalanche speed).
Goal of the research	The sensor network measures the displacement/velocity field inside a flowing bulk. Before the material is released, the sensor nodes are spread onto the surface or inside the material. After release, the information of each node is monitored to determine the flow structure. The main tasks are twofold: constructing a sensor network and interpreting the data to build more accurate fluid-dynamics models.
Expected results	Deployment of a sensor-network under real conditions to predict the risks of avalanche
Measure of success	The SLF deployed a network of 100 nodes in an Alpine area to predict the risks of avalanche. The results obtained by the sensors, as well as the treatments using fluid-dynamics models, allow us to obtain valid results with an error margin of 20% during a season (01.11 to 30.04).

as well as to propose new claims. The ideation process should be as smooth as possible to guarantee the best performances.

A trader is able to add a new claim, in connection with their field of research, to test their research proposal on the market. To find a way in-between a peer-review process and a flood of claims, a fee mechanism could be put in place. With such a mechanism, a trader has to pay a fee (in the market's money) to submit a new claim. Furthermore, they should also earn a percentage of the shares at the settlement of their claim. This process guarantees a low entry barrier on the market for new ideas and thus promotes the sharing of new ideas and concepts on the platform. We defined an IPO process in four stages: (1) claim proposal, (2) discussion on the formulation of the claim, (3) price determination, by putting limit orders on the claim and (4) opening of the trades on the market (section 4.7).

5.5.3. A simplified trading interface

In response to the evaluation of our first implementation, we decided to move from the traditional stock exchange interface. This unnecessarily increased the complexity of the trader's experience as stated by a trader at GE: *I felt that the tool obfuscates the very opinions it seeks to gather due to the inherent complexities of market behaviour.* [5] Our new trading interface moves away from the traditional stock exchanges interfaces. It consequently allows an easier use for uninitiated people. Thus, it was necessary to carefully make design choices in order to avoid an over-simplification of the interface. This could have tended to transform our prediction market into a voting or polling system. We then decided to keep the main concepts of purchase and sale, as well as limit and market types of orders (Figure 5.4). Moreover, in the current version, we keep the concept of quantity. It would be interesting, in future research, to develop an interface that allows the trader to determine a probability and then to suggest an order (quantity and price) that can make the market price evolve to the expected new price.

5. `http://www.grcblog.com/?p=378`

5.5.4. A combination of group and individual sessions

Various incentive mechanisms were discussed in section 4.7. However, to provide a good participation rate on scientific or technology prediction markets, we accompanied the experiment by group sessions. As stated by LaComb et al. [96], the group sessions during the launching of the market or in the course of the experiment, increased the interaction between the traders. Consequently and according to our experiments, it is recommended to set up such group sessions. Incentives such as iPods or other gadgets are not always sufficient to bring the traders on the market, as shown in our fourth experiment.

5.5.5. An automatic market maker

On this point, there is a consensus within the community. It is essential to have a market maker when using prediction markets in such contexts. However, we did not study, the use of other automated market maker mechanisms such as Pennock's dynamic pari-mutuel [126]. An inherent problem using automated market maker mechanisms is their tendency to act as a money pump if they are not correctly calibrated for the market. A thorough study concerning the calibration of these mechanisms not having been made yet, it was difficult for us to fully control it. However, as our markets were play-money based, this did not have a direct influence on the experiments.

5.6. Contribution > Five design propositions

In conclusion, our design science process, composed of four build-and-evaluate loops, supported with our artifact, led us formulate five propositions to design a predictions market for technological forecasting.

Proposition 1 A prediction market for technological forecasting should integrate a *standard framework to support claim formulation.* Using an indicator incorporated in the form of a price makes the evaluations comprehensible by all actors. Consequently, it is advisable to make sure that, independently of their activity, the traders have the same claims comprehension. Moreover, a structured framework helps in defining claims or structuring interviews with concerned people.

Proposition 2 A prediction market for technological forecasting should integrate an *easy IPO mechanism to support the innovation process.* The prediction market should allow researchers to test their research ideas among all actors, without needing a review process or preliminary validation. This direct access to the market removes internal barriers to innovation without requiring modification of the usual selection processes.

Proposition 3 A prediction market for technological forecasting should *occult the financial mechanisms to reduce the traders' learning curves and increase their incentive.* Observations resulting from our interviews showed that the researchers are by no means familiar with the underlying concepts such as limit orders necessary to play on a prediction market, which results in errors, and discourages them from playing on the market. This implies specific usability requirements on the human–computer interface.

Proposition 4 A prediction market for technological forecasting should *allow the combination of group sessions with individual sessions to increase the incentive of the traders.* Group sessions allow an evaluation of the portfolio to be obtained very quickly, generating a specific dynamic. Siemens used this configuration during one-hour meetings, but it could also be used in a distance synchronous trading way (e.g. by opening the market for one hour every month).

Proposition 5 A prediction market for technological forecasting should *integrate a market maker to increase the quality of the evaluation.* The market maker makes the market more reactive and fluid, allowing the traders to buy or sell each time new information is available. Thus the evaluation will aggregate more information, compared to a double auction market were the traders must wait for a similar offer to make the deal.

6. PM to assess R&D Portfolio Management [1]

Based on the promising results from the first iteration, this chapter discusses the adoption of prediction markets to partially support the R&D portfolio management process. Our findings are that prediction markets are powerful tools for addressing various issues encountered during the selection process.

6.1. Introduction

The R&D project portfolio management is a periodic activity that aims at optimizing the research effort of a company, while enabling it to select a portfolio that corresponds to its strategic objectives and without exceeding the resources available. Several studies have evaluated the practices in "Fortune 500" companies, finding that there is neither a single method nor a solution applicable to all companies [35, 102].

6.2. Usage

The most recent investigations showed that, to be effective, portfolio management must apply a mix of various qualitative and quantitative methods [32, 36]. However, the use of quantitative methods presents weaknesses,

1. The content of this chapter was partially published in [52]: C. Gaspoz. Prediction Markets As an Innovative Way to Manage R&D Portfolios, *15th Doctoral Consortium at CAiSE-2008*, Montpellier, France, 2008.

mainly for (1) selecting the right criteria, (2) collecting the data, (3) and negotiating the portfolio between the different stakeholders.

Many authors have proposed different frameworks for selecting R&D project portfolios [4, 32, 36]. The invariants of these different frameworks are: (1) maximizing the value of the portfolio, (2) achieving a balanced portfolio and (3) building strategy into the portfolio (Figure 6.1).

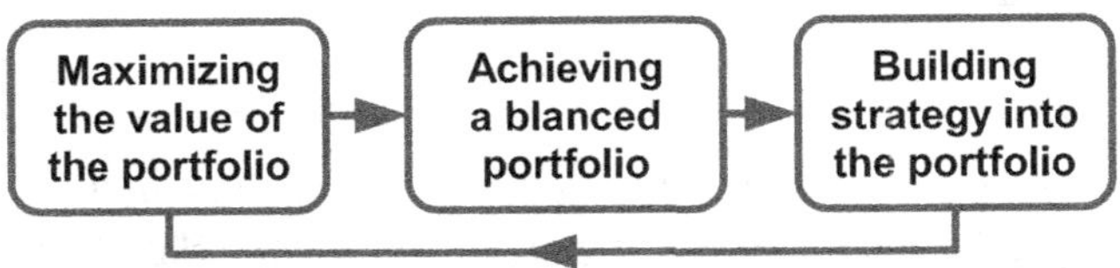

Figure 6.1.: The global R&D portfolio management process

Since many stakeholders, such as the different business units, are involved in the portfolio decision process, a "negotiation support system" could be the appropriate solution for speeding up the process. However, it will not significantly reduce the communication efforts. We suggest a paradigm shift with a new tool to address the portfolio management issues.

Our statement is that *a specifically designed prediction market could improve the R&D portfolio management process.* Prediction markets collect information coming from different actors, who trade on the market, and aggregate this information in an automatically negotiated equilibrium price, corresponding to the valuation of the project. All actors directly or indirectly linked to the project can trade (buy or sell) contracts concerning the projects, based on their own appreciation of the project. The traders are both the leaders and the teams of the project, and also the senior management, people from marketing and finance, as well as from all the other businesses units concerned with R&D. Their expertise within a specific company activity like research, but also marketing, sales, customer care or finance, will enable them to build their own opinion of the project, in the lighting of their particular field of activity.

The result of all aggregated appreciations will de facto include a multitude of implicit criteria related to all company activities. Such a market mechanism addresses the three weaknesses mentioned above: (1) no extra more criterion to be explicitly selected, (2) less data to be collected, and (3) fewer issues to be explicitly negotiated between actors. These three activities are implicitly replaced by the trading (buying and selling) of claims concerning the projects within the portfolio. In addition, prediction markets are a very powerful tool for discovering and aggregating information disseminated between many people. Thus, using prediction markets should not only make the whole process more effective, but also increase the quality of the decisions, based on more complete information.

6.3. Context > R&D portfolio management

The selection of a powerful project portfolio is a delicate exercise which requires wide competencies of strategic management and the associated tools regarding the objective criteria and also very good competencies in negotiation regarding the subjective criteria as well as the final choice of the portfolio composition.

> The portfolio decision process is characterized by uncertain and changing information, dynamic opportunities, multiple goals and strategic considerations, interdependence among projects, and multiple decision makers and locations.
> *Robert G. Cooper* [36]

Chien [32] provided an extensive literature review on portfolio selection and showed the inherent limitations of the existing R&D project selection models as follows: (1) inadequate treatment of multiple, often interrelated, evaluation criteria; (2) inadequate treatment of interrelationships among projects; (3) inability to handle non-monetary aspects; e.g. diversity among projects; (4) no explicit recognition and incorporation of the experience and knowledge of the R&D managers (i.e. the decision makers) and (5) perceptions by R&D managers that the models are difficult to understand and use.

Cooper et al. [36] showed that the combination of individually good projects does not necessarily constitute the optimal portfolio for the firm. This is often the case with firms having too many trivial projects and not enough projects that yield major competitive advantage. As seen in section 6.1, many authors proposed different frameworks for selecting R&D project portfolios [4, 32, 36, 159], resulting in three invariants: (1) maximizing the value of the portfolio, (2) achieving a balanced portfolio and (3) building strategy into the portfolio.

The two last stages are relatively well documented and supported by different frameworks, and use a wide range of visualization techniques such as bubble diagrams and scoring models. By contrast, the first stage is subject to a plethora of different methods requiring large investments in time and resources to collect the necessary data.

Liyanage et al. refer to more than 200 quantitative and qualitative methods for selecting R&D projects in their study [106]. The most often used methods are: the net present value (NPV), the expected commercial value (ECV), the productivity index, the options pricing theory and the dynamic rank-ordered list (Table 6.1). All these methods rely on various data that must be collected, evaluated or estimated before being used in the models. The principal issue concerning these data is their inaccuracy or unreliability, resulting in the financial methods yielding the worst portfolio results [36]. This is not so much from the fact that these models lack rigor; rather, it results from very poor data and forecasting in new product projects.

6.3.1. Selecting the right criteria

To be able to compare different projects at different stages with different goals, the senior managers first have to select the right criteria, applicable to all projects. These criteria may be financial like NPV or ECV, commercial like market shares, based on the consumed or planned resources, related to the pricing or the probability of technical success, etc. To select the right set of criteria, the company uses the experience of its senior managers but has to follow some intern guidelines, principally financial ones, needed

Table 6.1.: Principal methods used for selecting R&D projects

Method	Description
Net present value	Seeks to maximize the future net cash flows of the portfolio, minus the initial investment needed to develop the projects
Expected commercial value	Seeks to maximize the expected value, or expected commercial worth of the portfolio, subject to certain budget constraints
Productivity index	A variant of ECV in that it considers risks and probabilities of projects success
Options pricing theory	Like the ECV method, it seeks to maximize the expected value using the trade of options regarding the project's future outcomes
Dynamic rank-ordered list	Seeks to maximize the portfolio rank-ordering projects according to several concurrent criteria

for the budgeting process. This set of criteria can be elaborated iteratively by the experts with Delphi-like or NSS methods or be determined by quantitative methods. The output of this process is very important, influencing the whole selection of the portfolio.

6.3.2. Collecting the data

Once the criteria are determined, it is necessary to collect the quantitative information necessary for their evaluation. During the initial stage of the project, the lack of concrete information leads the various experts to make projections, estimates or extrapolations to quantify the various indicators, more reliable data being only available at a later time, according to the project advance. Consequently, their use of a sophisticated mathematical model has only little significance at the initial stage and could lead to very inaccurate results. However, this initial phase is of great relevance for the decision whether or not to incorporate the new project in the overall portfolio.

The second problem concerning the data collection is their constant update during the whole project life. Even if the data tend to approach reality as the project advances and becomes more concrete, their acquisition remains tiresome. Whereas certain data can easily be extracted from the company's reporting tools, others require a lot of work. Thus, for example, data concerning the acceptance of new technologies, future market shares, product lifespan, competitors' actions and so on must be the subject of a new study for each portfolio actualization. This renders the process inflexible and often leads managers to use obsolete data, having neither time nor resources to gather more up-to-date information.

6.3.3. Negotiating the evaluation

Since R&D portfolio management is often a team activity and involves several stakeholders (i.e. business units), the decision issues and positions are often the result of a negotiation process. Coupled with the previous comment on criterion selection, it means that R&D portfolio management could be considered as a multi-actor negotiation or multi-criterion decision-making process [26]. Several models have been proposed in the negotiation literature. Kersten [90] suggests a negotiation model with five phases:

1. search for arena and selection of communication mode (synchronous or not)
2. agenda setting (decision attributes)
3. exploring the field (best alternatives for negotiation agreement)
4. narrowing the difference and searching for the agreements (with compromises, offers and counter-offers, etc.
5. agreement assessment and fulfillment

This kind of model and the associated negotiation support systems (NSS) tools facilitate the communication activities. However, although they obviously speed up the process and eliminate ambiguities, they do not reduce the communication intensity. Our claim is that, with another paradigm, we could drastically reduce the communication effort itself, substituting the multi-stakeholder negotiation process by a market mechanism.

6.4. Evaluation

To evaluate this new usage of prediction markets, we choose to use an ex-ante evaluation, due to the fact that it is very complicated to design a good ex-post evaluation. To be able to run an ex-post evaluation, we would have to build and test our market in a real-life context, but this would only be possible in an artificial situation. Indeed, evaluating such a market would imply running two experiments in parallel: a traditional R&D portfolio management technique and a prediction market. Moreover, we would need to develop and pursue all projects from both methods to be able to evaluate the correctness of the two approaches. Such an experiment would considerably exceed the boundaries of our research.

Inspired by Pries-Heje et al. [136], we made an ex-ante evaluation, i.e. on the design of our prediction market, regarded as a new process to manage R&D portfolios. Furthermore, we followed a naturalistic approach for this evaluation. In the following sections, we present the issues solved by our new process, an extensive justification based on past results from the literature and finally a proposal to incorporate our new process in the global R&D portfolio management process.

6.4.1. Issues addressed by prediction markets

Using a prediction market in parallel with qualitative methods would allow managers to obtain discrete data in a relatively economic and fast way. In addition, by their nature, prediction markets render not only one discrete value at a given time, but also the evolution of this equilibrium value during the whole project life, making it much more significant than a simple discrete value.

Selecting the right criteria

Spann et al. [156] evaluate the potential use and different design possibilities as well as the forecast accuracy and performance of virtual stock markets compared to expert predictions for their application to business forecasting. Furthermore, they propose a new validity test for prediction market forecasts. Plott and Chen [133] analyze markets as information gathering tools, report on the deployment of such an information aggregation mechanism (IAM) within Hewlett-Packard for the purpose of making sales forecasts, and show that IAMs performed better than traditional methods employed within Hewlett-Packard.

Used for R&D portfolio management, prediction markets enable – once the project proposal has been released – the creation of a new claim tied to the project, which will be released on the market. As of this time, all actors directly or indirectly linked to the project can trade (buy or sell) contracts concerning the project, based on their own appreciation of the project. It thus becomes easy to obtain a discrete evaluation of each project, allowing them to be classified in order of importance or as clusters.

Using implicit comparison criteria, prediction markets enables the combining of a great diversity of appreciation criteria in a completely transparent way and to aggregate them in a price, representing the actual consensus on the claim. This is particularly true when an ontology, shared by all actors, is used to describe the project claims, enabling each trader to have the same frame of reference.

Collecting the data

Wolfers and Zitzewitz [171] describe early experiments concerned with prediction markets, raise some market design issues and conclude with some evidence as to the limitations of prediction markets. They also find that prediction markets prices typically provide useful (albeit sometimes biased) estimates of average beliefs about the probability of an event occurring [173]. Chen et al. [29] propose and experimentally verify a market-based method to aggregate scattered information so as to produce reliable forecasts regarding uncertain events; they empirically demonstrate that nonlinear aggregation mechanisms vastly outperform both the imperfect market and the best informed traders. Wolfers and Zitzewitz [173] show that the success of the prediction market in generating trade depends critically on attracting uninformed traders. To test how much extra accuracy can be obtained by using real money versus play-money, Servan-Schreiber et al. [146] set up a real-world on-line experiment showing that play-money markets performed as well as real money markets. They speculate that real-money markets may better motivate information discovery while play-money markets may yield more efficient information aggregation.

In an R&D portfolio management context, prediction markets enable each actor, at any time, to integrate their private information by buying or selling contracts according to the difference between the equilibrium price and their own confidence. In this manner, the equilibrium price, while undergoing constant adjustments, will gradually incorporate more and more information due to the aggregating mechanism of the market. The trader's goal being to maximize their personal performance on the market, they will try to make profit each time they are in possession of information enabling them to adjust their position. To motivate them to be reactive, the prediction market enables the company to rank the traders obtaining the best performances, performances that can be rewarded by the company in the form of prizes or bonuses.

Finally, the use of prediction markets for R&D allows the solving of another problem concerning the portfolio maximization: the update of the data. Very often, data cannot be regularly updated in terms of the portfolio reviews, and the senior management has to deal with progress reports on which to base their analysis. With prediction markets, the quote of the contract fluctuates throughout the whole project life, after each transaction carried out by the traders. Thus, any modification of an internal or external factor related to the project will initiate a buy or sell order by the actor in possession of new information. This transaction will make the price evolve to a new equilibrium. In this manner, the senior managers can base their decision not only on the contract's price at a given time, but also on its evolution over a given period. This concept of the continuity of the evaluation also allows a better comparison between projects since in addition to one discrete value, it provides a comparison of the trend of the price of each project, enabling them to discover which projects are in a growing or declining phase.

Using a relatively basic mechanism, based on the buying and the selling of contracts, prediction markets can aggregate very efficiently, and in real time, the information disseminated between a wide range of actors, making superfluous the implementation of a specific actualization process. In addition, this quote not only represents the actualized consensus concerning the value of the project, but also represents the evolution of this consensus during the whole project life.

Negotiating the evaluation

Prediction markets can incorporate various trading mechanisms. Whereas the simplest use a continuous double auction mechanism, the most advanced implement a market maker in order to fluidize the transactions and to optimize the information aggregation mechanism. Various market maker mechanisms are studied in the literature. After introducing market scoring rules, Hanson [75] considers several design issues, including how to represent variables in order to support both conditional and unconditional estimates, how to avoid becoming a money pump via errors in calculating probabilities, and how to ensure that users can cover their bets, without needlessly preventing them from using previous bets as collateral for future bets. Berg et al. [19] show how prediction markets can be used for decision support. Rhode and Strumpf [138] studied a century of manipulations of prediction markets. Their work suggests that it is difficult and expensive to manipulate prediction markets for more than short periods of time. Studies on TradeSport point out that manipulations are reverted within minutes by other traders.

On an R&D prediction market, the negotiation of each project's relative value is the result of the various sell or buy orders placed by the traders. These orders are processed by a market maker in a completely automatic way, allowing the carrying out of the transaction and the establishment of the new equilibrium price. Thus instead of using an inter-actors negotiation support system, we use a transparent system allowing each actor, at any time, to negotiate a new equilibrium price with the marketm maker.

In addition, as with the stock exchange portfolios, the traders do not rely on unlimited resources. Following this, their relative influence on the market will evolve according to their performance. Thus, the best-informed traders will benefit from the appreciation errors of the less informed ones or from those trying to manipulate the quotation to make a profit, allowing them, using the additional resources acquired, to increase their influence on the market. At the same time, relative to their losses on the market, the others traders will see their possibility of influencing the course reduced. For that reason and in spite of the number of significant actors, the equilibrium price is the result of a consensus between all the actors, according to their relative influence, not based on their position in the company, but on of their overall performance.

Using an automatic market maker, prediction markets enable continuous negotiation of the value of each project of the portfolio between all the actors, according to their relative influence on the market. In addition, this mechanism provides a greater cohesion of decision-making since the price at a given time is the result of the negotiation of all actors concerning the advisability of carrying out a given project.

6.4.2. Various experiments in related fields

We have seen in section 6.3 some issues affecting the R&D portfolio management process. We also saw in section 6.4.1 how a carefully designed prediction market could solve or ameliorate some of these issues.

Currently, there are no studies reporting on experiments in this field. However, some studies (see below) present very similar applications, such as new product development, idea generation and group decisioning and to create and evaluate new product ideas. We will therefore compare three different studies on applications of prediction markets in related fields and will highlight their principal design choices. This overview will then enable us to determine the necessary design choices to implement a prediction market for R&D portfolio management.

Securities trading of concepts (STOC)

The securities trading of concepts (STOC) was developed and used by Chan et al. [27] in 2002 to collect consumer preferences on product concepts. Consumers are asked to express their preferences for new product concepts by trading virtual securities, i.e. claims. STOC could be used to complement or replace traditional methods of collecting this information. Well known and used methods are surveys, conjoint analysis, concept tests or focus groups.

STOC could improve these methods in four ways: (1) *accuracy*—participants are motivated to express their opinion as often as needed, (2) *interactive learning*—participants not only act on their own behalf, but adapt it from the valuation of other participants, (3) *scalability*—STOC markets can handle an unlimited number of participants and products and (4) *unarticulated needs*—like other computer-supported tools, the STOC market can handle *virtual products* [39] such as movie scripts or fashion items that cannot be handled by traditional surveys.

Design Chan et al. ran multiple trading experiments to predict the market share of nine concept bike pumps and eight crossover vehicles (Table 6.2). Participants were asked to evaluate the company share price if a company was going public with its product, assuming that all companies have the same cost structure. In this case, all factors other than the quality and desirability of the products could be ignored in valuing the stocks.

Traders were asked to trade for 10 minutes in a trading room or 60 minutes over the Internet. Participants were not allowed to submit their own product idea or attributes. They had to trade on 11 predefined claims representing various bike pump designs.

Results The results of the experiments—the closing market price of each share—were compared with a survey study, and Chan et al. found significant correlation between the results of the two methods.

The Imagination Market

The Imagination Market was developed inside GE as a support tool for idea generation and group decisioning by LaComb et al. [96]. Participants were able to trade shares of technology ideas over the course of three

Table 6.2.: STOC market design

Participants	18/26* MBA students
Initial claims	11
IPO	Not available
Final payout	Sum of cash and total worth of the stocks at the closing market price
Money	Play-money
Market duration	10/60* minutes
Initial grant	Cash and shares for each claim
Anonymity	Through self selected username
Short-selling	Not allowed
Incentives	Prizes for the three best players
Information	All information is available on the STOC market (product description and attributes)
Trading	CDA
Evaluation	Comparison with survey study

*Respectively for the first/second experiment

weeks, resulting in the market identifying the "best" idea as the highest-priced security. Based on the observation that new ideas could emerge from anywhere within the organization, LaComb et al. tried to use a prediction market for collaborative brainstorming and idea ranking. Such a market could solve some recurring issues in idea generation and group decisioning such as the need for simultaneous participation by all participants.

LaComb et al. [96, 97] define the most important features for such a system as: (1) support for large, globally distributed teams with potentially thousands of contributors, (2) continuous idea contributions and ranking, (3) idea spring boarding, allowing contributors to be inspired by ideas from others, (4) responsiveness to new information such as the release of a new product line by a competitor and (5) correct ranking of ideas by participants. Furthermore, they added three more constraints to foster participation: (1) real-time feedback on ideas as they are generated, (2) visibility of the ideas and the process to all contributors and (3) consensus building, where all participants have a voice in the ranking process.

Design LaComb et al. ran the Imagination Market for three weeks, with employees from GE's Computing and Decisioning Sciences Technology Center (Table 6.3). The market started with five preselected ideas and ended with a total of 62 ideas. Participants were asked to judge each idea by whether it would: (1) have a high monetary impact to one or more GE businesses, (2) utilize advanced technology compatible with GE's focus areas, (3) demonstrate impact within 13 years and (4) be focused on growth-related ideas. In a second experiment [157] they slightly adapted their design, and participants where asked to evaluate how closely ideas fitted the criteria. This approach allowed participants to not only evaluate ideas in a similar manner to each other, but to use criteria that management would ordinarily use to evaluate ideas. The criteria were: (1) ideas that our customers will value, (2) ideas that will produce the best return on investment and (3) ideas that should be included for funding next year.

Table 6.3.: Imagination Market design

Participants	85 employees
Initial claims	5
IPO	All securities IPO'd 100 shares at $50
Final payout	Volume weighted average price (VWAP) during the final five trading days
Money	Play-money
Market duration	3 weeks
Initial grant	Cash plus a weekly cash allowance
Anonymity	Trader id
Short-selling	Allowed
Incentives	Prizes for the best players, lottery, group sessions
Information	Blogs to share information or discuss the ideas
Trading	CDA
Evaluation	Independent ranking of ideas by 11 members of the leadership team

Results The results of the experiments—the VWPA of each share—were compared with an independent ranking of ideas by 11 members of the leadership team, and LaComb et al. found that the market and the leadership team did not differ in their rankings of the securities. Furthermore, the Imagination Market generated more ideas than those methods that they had been used in the past, such as brainstorming and suggestion boxes.

Creating and evaluating new product ideas with idea markets

Soukhoroukova et al. [154] proposed the concept of idea markets as a new method of creating and evaluating new product ideas. The findings were that the creation and evaluation of new product ideas are influenced by (1) a large number of ideas and idea creators involved, (2) group decisions instead of individual decisions, and (3) methods that combine the creation of ideas with their evaluation. Combining these three factors, idea markets should be able to accurately support these processes.

Current methods utilized for idea creation and evaluation differ according to the tasks of idea generation (creation, evaluation or both), the number of participants and the degree of interaction among participants. Idea markets are characterized by an integration of a large number of participants, their interaction and the combination of both tasks, namely idea creation and evaluation.

Design Soukhoroukova et al. ran a real-world idea market for five weeks at the beginning of 2006 involving 642 participants from all hierarchical levels in a high-tech company (Table 6.4). The idea market consisted of three categories to explore the level of task specificity best for idea markets (a) new technologies for the company, (b) new product ideas for a specific product category and (c) innovative product and business ideas for the company. For category (a), the price of an idea stock reflected the *estimated percentage of revenues influenced by the respective technology in ten years*. In category (b), the price of an idea stock depended on the *estimated number of units that will be sold of such a product in ten years*. Category (c) was a miscellaneous category for product and business ideas of any kind, of which the *ten best ideas* were worth $100, and $0 otherwise [154].

Results The idea market actively evaluated the idea stocks, but the consensus between the evaluation of the idea markets, the one of senior management, the individual participants and the expert committee is only moderate. There were 252 idea were submitted, more than half coming from participants not involved in new product development. Of these, 100 ideas went through the screening and IPO process and were actively traded on the market. The results suggest that idea markets are a promising method for supporting the idea generation process.

Table 6.4.: Idea market design

Participants	642 employees
Initial claims	10 ideas collected by the innovation team
IPO	Expert screening with uniform price IPO mechanism
Final payout	Expert committee determine a pay-off value for each idea stock
Money	Play-money
Market duration	36 days
Initial grant	Cash
Anonymity	Through self-selected username
Short-selling	Not allowed
Incentives	Prizes for the best players
Information	All information is available on the market with the possibility of adding external links
Trading	CDAwMM
Evaluation	Management survey with 25 senior managers

First findings from past experiments

We studied the various design of STOC, information and idea markets mentioned above, which are all based on the same principles with very little differences. So, for the purpose of this comparison, we will use the common denomination "prediction market" for all of them.

All studies found that prediction markets are able to accurately determine the value of a project or an idea. Moreover, they are particularly well designed to leverage new ideas, projects or collaboration among the disparate group of employees. Therefore, by analogy, they should be able to accurately assess the value of R&D projects, which are—in effect—the formalized result of an ideation process.

Using a participative process to leverage the knowledge about R&D projects in an organization—aggregating bits of widely dispersed information in a non-intrusive manner—leads to the same results as traditional methods. In addition, a prediction market should support no restrictions in the number of participants and duration but should also support an IPO process to integrate new research ideas.

6.5. A proposal

Retaining the most significant design choices from the previous section, we can extrapolate the design characteristics of a prediction market for R&D portfolio management, as presented in Table 6.5.

6.5.1. Main design choices

Based on our previous experiments (chapter 5) and on the results of Chan et al. [27], LaComb et al. [96] and Soukhoroukova et al. [154], we can derive the principal design factors of a prediction market applied to R&D portfolio management.

Table 6.5.: Main characteristics of a PM for R&D portfolio management

Characteristic	STOC	Imagination	Idea	R&D
Participants	18/26	85	642	open
Claim	product description	framework	free text	framework / ontology
IPO	no	yes (fixed price)	yes (screening)	yes (auction)
Final payout	market price	VWAP	experts	VWAP
Market duration	10/60 min	18 days	36 days	open
Initial grant	cash & shares	cash	cash	cash
Trading	CDA	CDA	CDAwMM	CDAwMM

Participants Various empirical studies [28, 33] as well as the results of the previous experiments tend to confirm that the size of the crowd playing on the market is not particularly relevant. However, the more players that are active on the market, the more liquidity they will bring in.

Claim None of the experiments uses a specific claim description. Claims are either traditional product descriptions with texts and pictures or ad-hoc frameworks resulting from a trial-and-error process. Based on our own results, presented in chapter 5, we would argue that a claim description based on a framework and ontology provides better results, allowing each participant to have the same understanding as others. The framework described in section 5.5.1 could be used without modification. Nevertheless, the underlying ontology should be adapted to the context of the company, mostly to reuse already shared ontology.

IPO The use or not of an IPO process is discussed in LaComb et al. [96] without a definitive statement in favor of its use. However, we tend to consider that such a mechanism could improve the overall investment in the market. As seen in Soukhoroukova et al. [154] half of the ideas were proposed by participants outside the traditional innovation process. Thus, opening the market to every idea seems to be beneficial. Nevertheless, it is important to avoid a flood of ideas by implementing an appropriate mechanism as discussed in section 5.5.2.

Final payout As discussed in Soukhoroukova et al. [154], the choice of the final payout should be carefully selected. We feel that any external intervention in the fixing of the market price or the payout would add bias to the results. Thus, previous studies as well as our own experiments tend to show that traders could be motivated to manipulate the market at the end of the trading period in order to maximize their portfolio's value. Therefore, it seems that a payout based on the VWAP of the final trading days would be the most appropriate, as used by Gruca et al. [65].

Market duration There are two underlying issues connected with the market duration. The most important is the quality of the results. Chan et al. [27] and Plott and Chen [133] ran prediction markets for short time interval (from 10 minutes to 1 hour) with good results. We can conclude that there is no minimum duration to take into account. The other issue is the engagement of the participants in the long term. If prediction markets like Hollywood Stock Exchange or Foresight Exchange succeed in keeping their traders engaged by continuously adding new claims, there is no guarantee that it will be the case in our configuration. LaComb et al. [96] and Soukhoroukova et al. [154] both ran experiments for longer periods with mixed results. LaComb et al. had to distribute more prizes and organize "trading parties" in order to keep the engagement of the participants to a supportable level. We suggest designing an experiment not exceeding a couple of weeks with a large collection of diverse incentives to provide more information on the effects of the measures used to motivate traders.

Initial grant We saw two different types of initial allocation. The most used in experiments was the allocation of a cash amount at the beginning of the game, with or without weekly allocations. This is easy to implement on each market type. The second solution is the allocation of a mix of shares and cash. This solution has the advantage that participants have to trade on every share available on the market. Thus, it could become unmanageable in markets with a large number of shares. Furthermore, there is no evidence that one solution has a significant effect on market accuracy [124]. As a design choice, we propose to use a cash-only initial allocation.

Trading As discussed in section 5.5.5 the use of a CDAwMM mechanism, and though Chan et al. [27] and LaComb et al. [96] did not use such a mechanism in their experiments, there is a consensus that an automated market maker improves the liquidity of the market without negative side effects on its accuracy.

6.5.2. Running a PM for portfolio

Let's look again at the main issues we should cover with our prediction market: (1) selecting the right criteria, (2) collecting the data, and (3) negotiating the portfolio between the different stakeholders. If we try to translate these issues into a roadmap for implementing prediction markets for R&D portfolio management it becomes:

1. Ask the right question of the participants to make sure that they all have an equal *comprehension* of the evaluation that they are asked to give.
2. Give enough *incentives* to motivate participants to reveal and aggregate their own private information on the market.
3. Manage enough *liquidity* on the market to ensure an optimal price equilibrium.

Comprehension The more participants we would like to involve on the market, the more attention should be given to this topic. In fact, restricting the market to a handful of participants sharing the same comprehension of the topic would probably result in a common perception of the task to be done. However, there is a major risk that the market would not be as effective as desired, because these participants would probably share the same belief on the outcome of the different shares. To avoid this, we should integrate "noise traders" on the market to add sufficient opportunities for the best informed traders to reveal all their information, continuously adjusting the market prices [82, 163, 6].

This is why we should take great-care with the editing of the claims' descriptions—using the previously developed ontology—and of the questions asked. From an R&D portfolio management perspective, we should consider the impact of the different projects on the company. Bitman and Sharif [22] propose using five perspectives to assess the portfolio's projects, allowing us to define the questions to be answered by the traders:

Reasonableness Can the project be successfully completed?

Attractiveness Will the employees want to take part in the project?

Responsiveness Are there any ethical, moral, environmental or legal considerations that make it especially attractive or, conversely, inadvisable to carry out?

Competitiveness In what ways and to what extent does the project improve the firm's capability and competency?

Innovativeness To what extent will the project help the firm to sustain its competitive advantage?

Incentive Many experiments—including those in chapter 5—suffered from the traders' lack of willingness to actively participate on the market. There are many factors influencing the engagement of traders in real-life experiments. The most important is the fact that they are not paid—in contrast to participants in experiments—to participate on the market, but to do their daily business. Siegel [147], CEO of Inkling Incorporated,[2] made extensive trials on incentive techniques to achieve a sufficient participation on the market. His main findings are:

Length of markets Should be a mix of long-term and short-term, or all short-term to guarantee enough activity

Loud and often Inform widely on the accurately predicted outcomes to raise the role of the prediction market from a game to a business tool

Ongoing communication Use blogs, newsletters or mailing-lists to catch the attention of the traders

Introducing new markets Regularly create new markets to maintain interest

Interesting insights Use the data created by people trading to discover other insights

Profile/interview your users Use the best players as vectors for your communication

Champions Make sure that the top management is involved, and communicate its involvement

Cash and prize incentives Lottery systems picking a winner from the pool of users are better than allocating a prize to the best trader

Competition as incentive Take advantage of the natural organizational rivalries that already exist

Exclusive access as incentive Create a separate marketplace for those who have performed particularly well

Run provocative markets Ask tough questions because these get people talking and create a good deal of interest

2. http://inklingmarkets.com

Let traders create their own markets Letting traders create their own markets motivates them to drive participation within their own market, attracting new traders

"The most important lessons learned is what incentives work are highly dependent on the existing culture of the company and the trading community" (Adam Siegel [147]). Due to the lack of empirical studies on this topic, we would suggest picking some elements, or using all of them, during the implementation of the prediction market, tailoring them to the company's culture.

Liquidity Comprehension and incentive having been solved, liquidity should not be an important problem. As seen before, the implementation of some trading mechanisms coupled with the right provisioning of traders' accounts—in cash and/or shares—should guarantee enough liquidity on the market. Furthermore, to the best of our knowledge, there are no experiments failing due to illiquid markets.

6.5.3. A roadmap

We have identified several design specifications as well as some implementation guidelines. These can be summarized in a roadmap for running prediction markets for R&D portfolio management.

1. Carefully select the traders among the stakeholders. If in doubt, select them all.
2. Formulate the claims and their evaluation criteria in order to make them unequivocal for all trader.
3. Design the market following the design principles presented in section 6.5.1.
4. Publicize your market through multiple communication channels. Use key players to support your message.

5. Start the market, allocating each of the traders a sufficient endowment to express their opinion.
6. Manage the market, communicating results, adding new shares, distributing prizes, organizing trading sessions.
7. Close the market by paying the traders according to the chosen payoff function and distribute more prizes.
8. Ask the management to give a feedback on the results of the market: are they useful for the company, what will be used, etc.

This roadmap is a short summary of our main findings and propositions resulting from our experiments and an extensive literature survey. As we chose to use an ex-ante evaluation for our new R&D portfolio management process, we are confident that this approach should successfully solve some issues of the traditional R&D portfolio management process, noting that these guidelines should be carefully challenged and adapted to each particular context.

6.6. Contributions

In this chapter, we designed a new R&D portfolio management process supported by an extensive use of prediction markets. As we saw in the previous sections, using a prediction-market-supported process in this field solves three main issues encountered by traditional R&D portfolio management processes.

1. selecting the right criteria
2. collecting the data
3. negotiating the portfolio between the different stakeholders

Overcoming these issues, using a simple tool, should improve the overall decision process: the decisions will be more accurate, and the main stakeholders will identify with those decisions.

Moreover, we present the main design factors that should be retained to build such a tool as well as giving a roadmap to implement such a process.

Finally, we make some recommendations using such a process to support the R&D portfolio management activity. However, we were not able to set up an experiment to test the success of our approach in a real-life context mainly due to the boundaries of our research area and the difficulties of finding a context where both traditional and prediction-market-selected projects could be pursued to their end, to be able to measure their individual success.

7. PM for Technology Foresight

The final iteration of our design process summarizes our previous findings and studies the adequacy of prediction markets for technology foresight[1]*. To support our idea, we benchmarked a prediction market with an MCDM approach. We then developed a comparison framework to highlight the characteristics of prediction markets and MCDM. This led us to summarizing key success factors for each of our approaches.*

7.1. Introduction

According to McKeen and Smith [115], one of the critical issues in IT management is to "situate the challenges facing the IT managers regarding emerging technology...". This requires companies to adopt a systematic process to stay up to date and to assess new technology for potential integration into modern organizations. Different management tools and techniques have been proposed in the scientific community and in the literature (scenario planning, technology roadmap, ROI and real option) but few of them have been widely adopted by companies.

This chapter focuses on two approaches that support the assessment and foresight of new technology in order to evaluate how businesses can take advantage of them: *multi-criteria decision-making (MCDM)* and *prediction markets*. In addition, we also propose a number of critical success factors that make one or other of the approaches more appropriate to be used

1. The content of this chapter was partially published in [54]: C. Gaspoz, J. Ondrus and Y. Pigneur. Comparison of Multi-criteria and Prediction Market Approaches for Technology Foresight, *13th Conference of the Association Information and Management (AIM)*, Paris, France, 2008.

in certain corporate conditions. We used and validated both approaches during the assessment of mobile payment technologies.

7.2. Usage > Presentation of the approaches

The two selected approaches for our research differ in many aspects. Before comparing them, we briefly describe their aim and context of usage.

7.2.1. MCDM: A management science approach

MCDM methods aim at supporting decisions in an effective way by analyzing a problem using either quantitative (e.g. cost, weight) or qualitative (e.g. quality of service, beauty) criteria simultaneously. The idea behind MCDM methods is not to find the single optimal solution (like a mathematical programming model) but rather to try to determine which solutions are the closest to *optimal* in terms of the various criteria and to see how they compare with existing solutions. To collect the data, decision-makers (i.e. experts) need to express their preferences by evaluating the alternatives and giving each criteria a weight.

Previous research indicates that MCDM methods are not only used for decision-making but also for technology foresight [142]. Three distinct phases of the decision have been characterized by Simon [149]. These are intelligence, design and choice. Bui [25] argues that MCDM methods usually focus on the final two phases. In our case, the objective is to use MCDM methods for the intelligence phase of the decision process. The idea is to examine the current environmental conditions and uncover potential future issues before the establishment of the decision.

7.2.2. Prediction markets: an emerging approach

As discussed in chapter 2, prediction markets enable everybody to trade by aggregating the information disseminated among all actors in a corporate crowd (e.g. employees, business partners). Furthermore, they allow actors to trade based on their own assumptions, without worrying about hierarchy or other social pressures. Hanson [72] made the assumption that prediction markets should improve the progress of science based on the absence of social, economic and political pressures.

Previous research has also shown that the information disseminated in the crowd is not the same as the information reported to the hierarchy. This difference was partially explained by the anonymity of the traders on the prediction market and by the reward process, based on the best performances (i.e. the quality of the information supplied).

7.3. Context > Related work

Several authors studied the choice and usage of technological forecasting methods in different types of organizations. Porter et al. [135] introduced technology futures analysis (TFA) as a field grouping all forms of analyzing future technology and its consequences. After presenting and classifying more than 50 methods, they present two scoping issues of TFA: the content issues (i.e. time horizon, geographical extent, level of detail) and the process issues (e.g., participants, decision process, study duration, resources available).

Martino [114] presents a review of recent advances in technological forecasting based on eight methods and shows the resulting possibilities from these new approaches.

Presenting the implementation issues of technology intelligence systems, Savioz et al. [143] note the importance of the specific character of each organization in setting up such a system.

Levary and Han [101] identify six main factors affecting technological forecasting and the choice of a method: (1) money available for development of technology, (2) data availability and validity, (3) uncertainty surrounding the success of technological development, (4) similarity of proposed and existing technologies, (5) number of variables affecting the development of technologies and (6) prerequisites for use of specific technological forecasting methods.

Lichtenthaler [104] conducted an exploratory case study research in leading multinationals that identified the most influential contingency factors for the selection of technology intelligence methods and assessment forms.

He [103] also presents the importance of the type of coordination of the technology intelligence process (structural, hybrid and informal) as well as the selection of information sources in the choice of a specific method.

We found that none of this previous work elaborates a comparison of selected approaches with their strengths and weaknesses related to their contextual implementation.

In this chapter, we propose to establish a comparison framework based on characteristics derived from past research previously presented. This framework aims at helping us to compare our two approaches and identify their key success factors.

7.4. Evaluation > Benchmark

To evaluate the usage of prediction markets in a technological forecasting context, we made a benchmark between prediction markets and MCDM, comparing the results of both methods. This benchmark was made in the field of mobile payment technologies and was supported by a dedicated comparison framework inspired by [104].

7.4.1. Design of the artifacts

In order to support our research, we designed two artifacts implementing the MCDM and prediction market approaches. As a research methodology, we adopted a design science paradigm and rigorously followed the recommendations prescribed by Hevner et al. [84]. More details about the artifact implementing MCDM methods can be found in earlier work [119].

MCDM: A group decision support system

The requirements for a multi-actor multi-criteria analysis are not easily fulfilled, as a large amount of data has to be collected, computed and visualized. Obviously, a digitization of the processes is necessary. In other words, we decided to use an IT artifact (a group decision support system, GDSS) integrated with the processes of an MCDM approach. As none of the existing MCDM tools surveyed encompassed the features needed, we designed a new and original prototype with unique characteristics required for our research. We concentrated our efforts on the development of an interactive user interface in order to improve data collection, computation and visualization.

Our prototype, PylaDESS, implements side-by-side two formal MCDM methods: ELECTRE I [11] and the weighted sum model (WSM) of Fishburn [47]. To collect the data, we selected an interactive process based on the "Pack of Card" technique proposed by Simos [150] and later improved by Pictet and Bollinger [130]. We programmed this technique in PylaDESS in order to facilitate data collection. Experts can evaluate technologies using a five-value scale – weak (1), fair (2), average (3), good (4), excellent (5) – for each criterion they estimate as relevant.

To improve the visualization and analysis of the data, we implemented many different data cross-analysis modules. All of these features make PylaDESS a unique MCDM tool to support multi-actor and multi-criteria analysis.

The iterative and incremental development of the IT artifact was done in the laboratory, and its testing was organized in a real environment. The design iterations allowed us to better manage the different constraints encountered during the analysis. In total, three distinctive iterations have been conducted. First, the artifact has been used in the back-office for manual data input and computation the data. During the second design iteration, the artifact was used by the experts to collect the data with a card game and give real-time feedback of the results computed. The third iteration consisted of using the artifact as a group support system in a round-table setting. During each of these iterations, numerous improvements were made in order to adapt the artifact to each context with its constraints.

Prediction market : e-trading market

As the technology foresight activity partially corresponds with the assessment of projects in an R&D portfolio, we chose to keep the same design constraints as described in chapter 6. The main difference lies in the definition of the portfolios. In the previous case, traders had to evaluate the "value" of each project in an R&D portfolio, given that there were no constraints on the number of projects selected. In this case, we have a portfolio of multiple technologies, but the outcome had to be unique—it is a winner-takes-all market. We summarize some key design constraints in Table 7.1.

As prototype did not support multiple winner-takes-all markets at that stage, we decided to use a different platform for this experiment. After a brief survey of the different marketplaces, we chose to use the InklingMarket[2] prediction market for our experiment. At the time of our experiment, it supported all our design constraints, as presented in Table 7.1. Furthermore, as discussed in section 5.5.3, they followed the same idea—removing the stock market concepts from the trading interface—which resulted in a very intuitive trading interface as seen in Figure 7.1.

2. http://inklingmarkets.com

Table 7.1.: Design constraints of the prediction market

Design	Constraint
Trading	MSR
Final payout	Sum of cash and total worth of the stocks at the closing market price
IPO	Not available
Initial grant	Cash (play-money)
Short-selling	Allowed
Shares type	Winner-takes-all

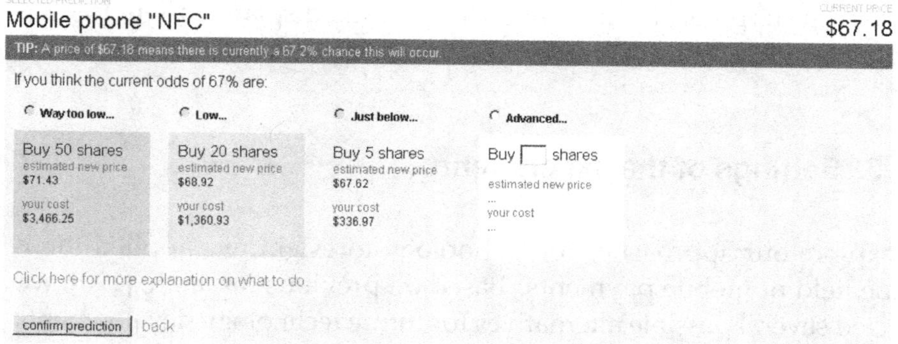

Figure 7.1.: Trading interface at InklingMarkets

The only weakness of the platform, at the time of the experiment, was its inability to specify a payoff function. So we had to use a final payout based on the sum of the cash and the total worth of the stocks at the closing market price in place of a VWAP, which could have been better, as proposed in section 6.5.

Comparison of the artifacts

The designed artifacts are quite different in their nature. PylaDESS is a standalone application coded in the Python programming language. It runs on most popular operating systems (MS Windows, Mac OS X and GNU/Linux). In terms of specific algorithms to compute the data, it implements two formal MCDM methods and produces visual outcomes (rankings and outranking graphs). Moreover, there are different visualization modules to conduct cross-data analysis. More details of PylaDESS features can be found in [119].

The prediction market architecture requires a web server and an Internet connection. The user interface is based on web standards such as HTML, which is compatible and reachable with any computer using a web browser. It supports buy and sell operations and displays current trading information (e.g. price, volume).

7.4.2. Settings of the experiments

To explore our approaches for technology foresight, we applied them in the field of mobile payments. Based on previous research, [120], we selected several possible alternatives for future technology developments in the Swiss mobile payments market.

In order to conduct a foresight process, we assessed current payment technologies and added possible future technologies. By mixing both current and future technologies, we were able to estimate more precisely the impacts of future trends based on the existing market conditions.

For the technology alternatives, we selected three types of cards: (i) SmartCards (chip-based), (ii) contactless cards (RFID-based), and (iii) magnetic cards (with magnetic strips). We also included two phone-based technologies, one using a phone remote network (e.g. GSM, GPRS) and another one based on phone proximity networks (e.g. Bluetooth, infrared). In a second phase we added an upcoming technology, near field communication (NFC). This technology is a fusion of the mobile phone and the contactless card. More information about RFID and NFC can be found in [168]. A summary with examples of the technologies and their uses is presented in Table 7.2.

MCDM: Visiting Swiss experts

During a first phase, we assessed the current technologies present on the Swiss market. We started this phase in November 2005 and finished it in May 2006. We selected 20 of the major companies involved in payments in Switzerland and visited each of them once or twice; depending on how much time they could give us.

The structured interviews lasted on average between half an hour and an hour, sometimes more. In general, we had between one and three experts representing the companies. All selected experts were leaders of mobile payments projects in their respective companies.

During the interviews, we used our computerized *Pack of cards* technique to elicit the preferences of the experts. The computerized process enabled direct input in PylaDESS and a real-time feedback of the results.

The second phase of the research (i.e., NFC assessment) consisted of a real-time group setting. This round-table session aimed at inviting all the companies that participated during the first phase of the project. There were 16 experts representing 14 different companies at the round-table in October 2006. This round-table had two distinctive parts. The first part consisted of a presentation of the results obtained previously. During the second part, we distributed individual forms for each expert to evaluate NFC using the five-value scale, as done before. After having inserted and

Table 7.2.: Different alternatives considered for our experiment

Description	Example	Use case
Magnetic card Card having a magnetic strip that is readable/writable when inserted in a card reader	Photocopy or gift cards	Use a gift card to pay at the register
SmartCard Card having a chip able to perform simple operations such as cryptography when inserted in a card reader	Bank cards such as EC, Postcard, VISA or Cash	Make a call in a public phone
Contactless card (RFID) Kind of smartcard whose chip is activated by the proximity of the reader's magnetic field	CampusCard, Mobility, Mobilis, Path, Skidata	Buy a coffee on the campus
Mobile phone "remote" Use the WAN capabilities of the mobile phone, using the operator's infrastructure	SMS/WAP	Buy a drink by SMS in a vending machine
Mobile phone "proximity" Use the PAN capabilities of the mobile phone, without using the operator's infrastructure	Bluetooth/WiFi	Send and print a photo from a mobile phone to a vending machine
Mobile phone "NFC" Integration of smartcard and contactless technologies (RFID) in a mobile phone	Suica/Edy	Pay for purchases by passing the phone near the register and typing a pin number on the phone

computed the data in PylaDESS, we immediately presented the results to the experts.

Prediction market: Gathering the crowd

We ran a prediction market based on the selected mobile payment technologies with 29 masters students in business information systems. The one-month experiment took place in May 2008. Twenty students were active on the platform. We recorded 390 trades representing 6291 shares from four markets containing 13 claims. Six of these claims were directly related to the technologies used in the MCDM approach as seen on Figure 7.2.

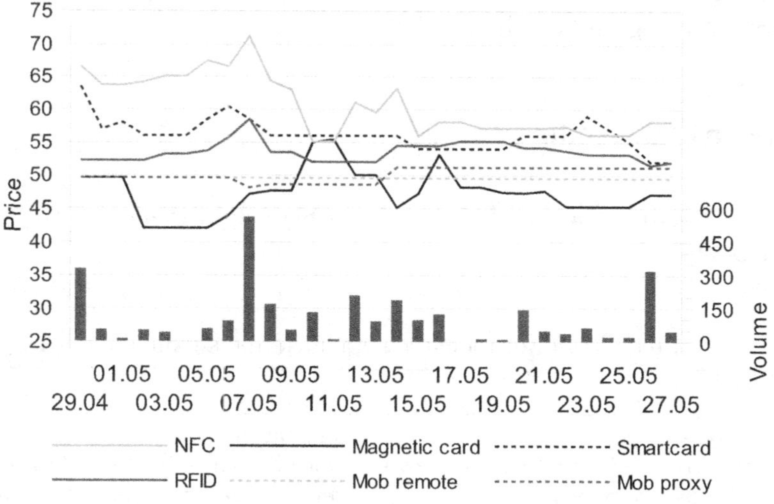

Figure 7.2.: Mobile payment technologies' quotes

The setup of the experiment took three working days. This includes the setup of the markets and user accounts. Furthermore, a presentation of the platform, its markets and claims was made in class. On the students' side, the investment is tightly linked to the number of trades made during the month. This includes the research of an investment opportunity based on information available to the trader, passing an order and looking at the new portfolio's value.

The incentive to play on the prediction market was a prize for the trader with the highest worth at the end of the experiment. This incentive alone was not sufficient to have a continuous trading volume on the market, so we introduced two short-term contracts during the experiment, resulting on trading peaks on the market.

Finally, to insure sufficient trades to extend the market accuracy, we used two strategies. First, we presented all markets and claims in details during the class, allowing students to ask questions about the claims and related issues. We completed this presentation with on-line material presenting each claim in detail, accompanied with presentation videos. Second, we used a market maker to allow the traders to quickly get their information aggregated on the market.

Comparison of the settings

As can be seen in Table 7.3, the settings for both approaches differ in several aspects.

Table 7.3.: Differences of experiments' settings

	MCDM	PM
Who	Selected experts	Students (crowd)
Where	One or two individual interviews with each company. One round-table for all the experts to meet, discuss the results and evaluate NFC	One group meeting to start the market and some trading activities. Later, the participants continue to trade alone anytime and anywhere.
When	Nov. 05 to May 06 + Oct. 06	May 08 (1 month)
How	Several months for setup, trips, phone calls, analysis	A few days for setup and analysis

A considerable effort is required for the MCDM approach compared to the PM approach, especially for the data collection process. Each company and its experts need to be met individually. The experts need more support while we elicited their preferences than the traders, who just buy or sell.

A multi-criteria analysis requires a relatively large amount of data to collect. The best way to proceed is to meet the experts face to face. The advantage of this direct contact is the personalized assistance and interaction during the whole process. This should prevent erroneous data sets.

In the prediction markets, the participation of the players is self-organized. This facilitates the overall management of the analysis. However, the success of the prediction market's outcome depends on the goodwill of the players to participate and trade without the pressure of the project managers.

Lastly, the first experiment lasted 8 months in 2005 and 2006, while the second lasted only one month in 2010.

7.4.3. Analysis of the results

MCDM: Ranking and outranking

From the results obtained, it was quite clear that card technologies were preferred to phones for payment purposes. The general ranking obtained with the WSM method shows that cards, especially smartcards and contactless cards, were preferred, with a high ranking.

Phone-based solutions remain in lowest positions of most rankings. This could be explained as mobile phone-based payment schemes are still in an early stage of development. Our results show that there is still progress to be made in terms of ease of use, cost, reliability and user/market acceptance (i.e., awareness). However, phone-based schemes already perform well in terms of flexibility and value proposition improvement. The three national mobile network operators consider value proposition improvement to be an important aspect, which explains why they believe that mobile phones have a future as a payment instrument. A complete description of the results of the first phase can be found in [120].

During the second phase, the results showed that NFC is highly valued. Its ranking is high and comparable to contactless and smartcards. It is clearly performing better than the other mobile phone technology tested in the first phase. A deeper analysis of the results is given in [121].

PM: Price of contracts

Given that the students were relatively well informed on this topic and made an intensive use of information disseminated, the results are the expression of a good consensus between the traders. We could observe that after a period of important variations during the first two weeks, the prices tended to reach a consensus at the end of the experiment while the volume of trades stayed at the same level.

On the mobile payment technologies market, we can distinguish two groups of claims. The first group, composed of NFC, SmartCard and RFID, was the most active in term of trades and all technologies reached a "price" over 50%. The second group consisted of claims with few trades and probabilities under 50%.

Our results indicated that NFC could be considered to be the next successful technology in the mobile payment field. The price history shows a regular adaptation to reach the consensus of 57.2%. We also saw a convergence of SmartCard and RFID technologies to reach a probability just above 50%.

At the other end of the scale the mobile phone proximity and remote technologies had few trades. The reason for this lack of interest could be the shortage of information or the lack of confidence of the traders. In any case, the results of these two claims are not significant.

Finally, magnetic card made a low score, supported by many trades. We can interpret this result as a clear sign of the gentle eviction of this technology on the payment market. Even thought the magnetic strips are still available on most cards, these cards also contain a chip, which put them in the SmartCards category.

Comparison of the results

The results of the prediction market are globally similar to the ones obtained with the MCDM approach. Table 7.4 summarizes these results. Due to the particularities of the methods used, we chose to not harmonize the two scales, prediction markets results expressing a probability, as MCDM results express the strength of various preferences.

Table 7.4.: Summary of the results (ranking)

MCDM	Prediction market
1. SmartCard (3.8/5)	1. NFC (57.16%)
2. NFC (3.6/5)	2. SmartCard (52%)
3. Contactless Card (3.6/5)	3. Contactless Card (52%)
4. Magnetic (3.3/5)	4. Phone proximity (51.20%)
5. Phone proximity (2.7/5)	5. Phone remote (49.51%)
6. Phone remote (2.7/5)	6. Magnetic Card (47.01%)

Two groups clearly emerged. The first group contains NFC, SmartCard and RFID, and the second one contains mobile phone proximity, remote and magnetic card.

The main difference discovered is the rank of technologies within the two groups. Magnetic card falls from rank four to rank six with the prediction market approach. After verification, the high trade volume compared to the two other technologies of the second group indicates that the result is significant in expressing the beliefs of the traders. A possible explanation of this lower ranking is the time lag between the two experiments. In the two years between the studies, most magnetic cards have been replaced by SmartCards in Switzerland. Also, the excellent performance of NFC in the prediction market could be explained by the increasing popularity and visibility of initiatives in Asia and the USA during this period.

7.4.4. Comparison and discussion

To compare our two approaches, we derived a framework based on the contingency factors developed by Lichtenthaler [104] and the individual factors affecting technological forecasting from Levary and Han [101].

Lichtenthaler found that the contingency factors influence the choice of assessment forms and technology intelligence methods used in multinationals. Levary and Han designed a framework to define the most appropriate forecasting method(s) for various combinations of the degree/extent of individual factors affecting technological forecasting.

The combination of the two groups of factors enables us to embrace the technological foresight activity globally and systematically from the organization characteristics to the information collection through the assessment process.

The resulting framework contains three main components: organizational factors, assessment properties and data attributes (Figure 7.3).

By organizational factors, we mean all factors determining the environment of the assessment process. These factors could be resource availability, the organization's internal communication culture or their decision-making style.

The assessment properties are the characteristics of the assessment conducted in a given organization. These properties could be the assessment's goal, the time horizon of the prediction or the uncertainty of the assessment field.

Finally the data attributes are the characteristics of the data needed for the technology forecast such as data quality and availability. We also distinguish between exogenous and endogenous data collection processes. In the exogenous processes, we do not worry about the provenance of the data and the channel used to collect them. The endogenous processes imply that we integrate a data collection process into the method. The main properties of each method are sumarized in Table 7.5.

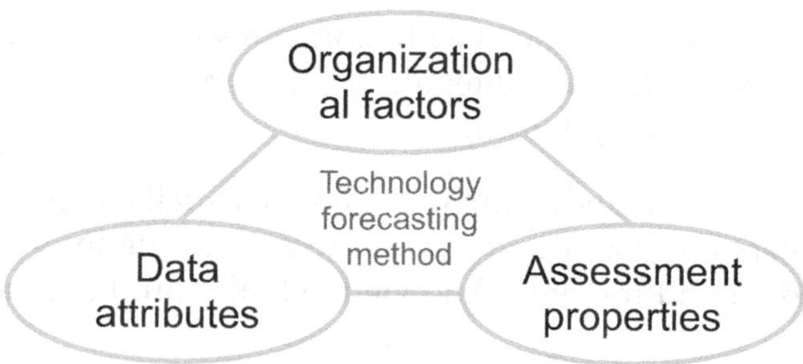

Figure 7.3.: Comparison framework

Organizational factors

These factors are specific for every organization. Even if they are not directly related to the assessment made, they will define its conditions and modalities. Often, they are implicitly embedded in the choice of a method. Time and human or financial resources dictate more or less the conditions of the assessment. In the case of limited resources, familiarity with the various methods will play an important role in restricting the choice of options.

The MCDM approach is well suited for organizations with formal and less participatory decision-making processes. This approach relies mainly on a few selected experts at the expense of the crowd. MCDM methods may be difficult to implement in more participatory organizations, as the number of possible participant is limited for practical reasons. Likewise, the experts need a good knowledge of the method, both for the assessment and the interpretation of the results.

To make efficient use of prediction markets, the organization must have a participatory and informal decision-making style. We need to open the market to the most players in order to aggregate more information. Due to their design, prediction markets do not require in-depth knowledge of the method. Participants just have two possible actions: buy or sell. Furthermore, the results are quite simple to interpret. Given the short implementation time of this method, it is well suited for fast-moving organizations or for organizations with limited resources. A challenge is to get participants to actively and regularly trade on their own, otherwise the results might not be significant.

In the MCDM approach, the actors involved are usually a set of selected and relevant experts who are motivated to participate in order to get access to the data and therefore knowledge that would augment their expertise.

In prediction markets, the participants can be anyone interested in technology but are not always experts—the crowd of Web 2.0. They constitute a community of players who are driven by the game and its financial profits. In contrast to the MCDM approach, prediction markets can easily indicate if players are good by considering the value of their portfolio and their total profit.

Assessment properties

The main property is the goal, which specifies whether to assess the current environment or to generate knowledge about the future. Properties also describe the nature of the information to be generated. Depending on the needs, we might require a static or dynamic picture of the trend studied.

The MCDM approach gives a posteriori results to support the resolution of a decision problem. At a specific time, the MCDM analysis draws a rather detailed picture of a situation benefiting from the granularity provided by the criteria. These criteria help to explain precisely the reasons for the outcome.

By contrast, prediction markets are excellent tools for longitudinal studies due to the inherent nature of the data collection process. However, they give the prediction (i.e. the claim's price) without further explanation. In other words, MCDM methods are detailed snapshots taken at a specific time and prediction markets are movies shot over a period of time, suitable for assessments requiring frequent or constant updates.

Data attributes

In MCDM, the data collection process is endogenous since experts elicit their preferences using criteria and alternatives previously established. As a result, a double risk of bias exists during the establishment of the criteria and alternatives and during the elicitation of the preferences. As the method cannot identify any bias introduced by experts, it may be necessary to couple MCDM with a Delphi analysis to avoid having too large disparities.

In the case of prediction markets, the data collection process is exogenous. Full interest is given to the assessment. The rest of the process is left to the crowd. Prediction markets are not affected by unreliable information, due to the aggregation mechanism. Prediction markets are well suited in cases where information is not available or is potentially unreliable.

Table 7.5.: Summary of the comparison factors

		MCDM	**Prediction markets**
organizational factors	decision-making style	formal	informal, participative
	resources restrictions	low	mid to high
	familiarity with the method	high	low
assessment properties	goal	scanning, forecasting	forecasting
	uncertainty	mid to high (in conjunction with other methods)	
	time horizon	mid (possibly long)	short to long
	type of results	static	dynamic
data attributes	availability	mid to high	not relevant
	origin	experts	crowd
	validity	relevant	not relevant

Key success factors

Based on the comparison, we propose some key success factors for MCDM and prediction markets applied in technology foresight. Our recommendations should support further explorations of these approaches.

MCDM methods are well suited for situations where a group of relevant experts want to challenge their own opinions in order to draw conclusions when technology trends are not easy to discern. For their part, prediction markets need a crowd ready to trade and share their beliefs. Their actions generate a prediction through an implicit data aggregation mechanism relying on information disseminated among the crowd. This works particularly well when the corporate crowd is familiar with the topic.

To set up an MCDM analysis, a facilitator should be hired to meet each expert individually. Face-to-face meetings are essential for sharing the results, as they are usually centralized in standalone software. Prediction markets only need a facilitator who can set up a claim on the platform. Then traders can play anytime and anywhere using a web browser. The major challenge of prediction markets is to gather a motivated crowd that will trade regularly.

The efforts required for the MCDM approach are rewarded with the assurance that the set of data collected is valid since the facilitator supervises the whole process. To overcome this issue in prediction markets, the crowd automatically regulates the market. Even if a trader introduces a bias in the market by their irrational actions, the crowd will neutralize it by doing opposite actions. At some point, the defective trader will be evinced, as their financial resources for trading will vanish.

MCDM methods are used when experts need to have a precise explanation of the phenomenon. The criteria, weights and evaluations are useful indicators for unveiling weak signals. In our case, the results were rankings and outranking graphs. Looking at the data collected, we could explain precisely how we reached these outcomes. As a result, a consensus could be reached after several rounds of analysis (i.e. Delphi).

The outcome of prediction markets is by nature a consensus of the crowd based on many rounds of trading. The aggregated results provide a simple but powerful indication of the probability that an event will occur. In addition, one can analyze the evolution of the trends by just looking at the history of the trading price. However, it is much harder to explain the behavior of the traders over time.

7.4.5. Conclusions

Despite similar results, both approaches revealed some benefits and demonstrated their complementarity. On one side, the MCDM approach bring an analytic explanation of the phenomenon by a controlled and criteria-based evaluation. On the other side, prediction markets provide a synthetic aggregation of numerous individual beliefs that is constantly adjusted and made available for everyone. Therefore, we could not claim that one is better than the other. Interestingly, we found that the drawbacks identified could partially be solved by selecting the best aspects of the two approaches.

For example, we could take consecutive snapshots during a given period of time to follow trends using a MCDM approach. Moreover, after few rounds of analysis, we could improve the data collection process by building an online user interface that would draw out the preferences without a face-to-face confrontation.

For prediction markets, the quality of the players could be ensured by opening the markets only to a community of practice, including its experts. Furthermore, the outcome of prediction markets could be enhanced by requesting more information about the actions of the players. The objective would be to monitor the behavior of the players in order to confirm that they are not just following the trend generated by the market.

7.5. Contributions

7.5.1. Efficiency of prediction markets

Comparing two different approaches for technology foresight—prediction markets and MCDM—we found that prediction markets are well adapted to solve technology foresight issues. Moreover, running an experiment assessing mobile payment technologies, we showed that prediction markets are as good as MCDM at assessing technologies, but are also more efficient.

We showed that, even in the presence of non-expert participants, prediction markets are faster to set up and more resource saving (time, education, costs) than MCDM, for achieving the same outcome.

These findings would help practitioners to design better technological forecasting tools and stakeholders to efficiently run their technology assessments or to improve their IT investment decisions.

7.5.2. Crowd challenging experts

Running these experiments with two different participants groups, enabled us to confirm that a crowd of graduate students is able to perform as well as selected and renowned experts. This could seem to be counter-intuitive at first sight, but it only confirms the findings from various experiments on prediction markets.

7.5.3. A comparison framework

In order to compare various approaches, we built a framework that contains three essential dimensions to differentiate technology foresight methods: (1) organizational factors, (2) assessment properties and (3) data attributes, as presented in Table 7.6.

Table 7.6.: Comparison framework

Organizational factors	decision-making style
	resources restrictions
	familiarity with the method
Assessment properties	goal
	uncertainty
	time horizon
	type of results
Data attributes	availability
	origin
	validity

Successfully used to differentiate prediction markets from MCDM, this framework will enable researchers to compare, and derive key success factors and particularities from, various technological forecasting methods. This framework will also support stakeholders in selecting the best adapted technological forecasting method to support their assessment needs.

Part IV.

Conclusions

8. Conclusions and final thoughts

This final chapter summarizes our findings by using two approaches. The first one presents our findings from a methodological point of view, following seven design guidelines from Hevner et al. [84]. The second approach presents our findings from a theoretical point of view, structured using Gregor and Jones's information systems design theory [60]. Then, we present some final thoughts concluding this book.

8.1. Conclusion

To conduct this research, we used a problem-solving process. We identified a problem to be addressed from the perspective of the environment, in this case, from various organisations. We then acquired knowledge and understanding of this problem during our subsequent iterations, building and running our artifact in various contexts. This knowledge was then used to refine our design during each iteration. This problem-solving process could be difficult to predict and its results are less readable than traditional research paradigms.

In order to structure our conclusion, we decided to follow two approaches. A methodological one, based on seven design guidelines from Hever et al. [84] and a theoretical one, based on Gregor and Jones's information systems design theory [60]. The two approaches are developed in the following sections.

8.2. A design science research process supporting technological forecasting

This section presents our conclusions from a methodological point of view, following the seven design guidelines of Hevner et al. [84]. These guidelines should help to show that we followed a complete design-science research process and addressed all its facets. However, these guidelines could not determine the quality of our research contributions. This will be addressed in the following section.

8.2.1. Design as an artifact

Design-science research must produce a viable artifact in the form of a construct, a model, a method or an instantiation

Our multiple iterations produced several artifacts in the form of constructs (claims), models (design factors typology, claim ontology), methods (R&D portfolio management process) and instantiation (MarMix). All these artifacts were instantiated and evaluated in various contexts.

8.2.2. Problem relevance

The objective of design-science research is to develop technology-based solutions to important and relevant business problems

During our interviews with other researchers, we identified the technological forecasting problem as an important issue still to be solved for practitioners. This was confirmed by our literature review, which allowed us to refine our research question to better address the current issue with our artifact.

8.2.3. Design evaluation

The utility, quality and efficacy of a design artifact must be rigorously demonstrated via well-executed evaluation methods

To evaluate our artifact, we used multiple methods during the various iterations. First of all, we made field studies with large groups of participants to test our prediction market design factors. We then used a descriptive approach which consisted of informed arguments originating from related work and literature to evaluate our portfolio management process. Finally, we used a benchmark to compare our artifact with a traditional forecasting method.

8.2.4. Research contributions

Effective design-science research must provide clear and verifiable contributions in the areas of the design artifact, design foundations, and/or design methodologies

The design artifact During this research, we developed MarMix, a prediction market tailored to support technology foresight, more precisely the first part of the R&D portfolio management process. This artifact was successfully used in various contexts and provided support for related contributions.

Foundations We made various contributions to the foundations. First, we contributed to the prediction market literature, documenting and testing a new application of this technique to technology foresight. Our research could help secure the adoption of prediction markets into the business toolbox. We also made contributions in the form of our design factors typology and our five design propositions, supporting designers in their development of innovative applications of prediction markets.

Second, we contributed to the negotiation support system (NSS) literature, presenting prediction markets as automated negotiation agents that could be instantiated to solve multi-actor multi-criteria problems. This contribution could help researchers in the NSS or decision support system (DSS) field to find new tools and techniques to solve issues in that field.

Third, we made an important contribution to the R&D portfolio management field, proposing an innovative way to solve some of the remaining issues. This contribution can help researchers to develop integrated ways to support the whole R&D portfolio management process, allowing practitioners to optimize and strengthen their process.

Design methodologies To assess the performance of both prediction markets and MCDM for technological forecasting, we contributed a comparison framework that enables us to characterize and evaluate various technological foresight techniques.

8.2.5. Research rigor

Design-science research relies upon the application of rigorous methods in both the construction and evaluation of the design artifact

To insure the rigor of our research we made extensive use of the available literature and models (knowledge base). Moreover, we exposed our results to other researchers in the field through peer-reviewed publications to strengthen our results.

8.2.6. Design as a search process

The search for an effective artifact requires the utilizing of available means to reach desired ends while satisfying laws in the problem environment

We adopted an iterative process to achieve the goal of our research. This process led us to build and evaluate our artifact in various contexts and environments. These multiple iterations led us to continuously refining our artifact based on the specifics of the context. They were also the way to test our research assumptions. Finally, to test whether we had found a satisfactory solution, we benchmarked our solution against an existing one.

8.2.7. Communication of research

Design-science research must be presented effectively both to technology-oriented and management-oriented audiences

We presented most of our results from the iterations in various scientific publications. These publications presented our findings from chapters 4 to 7. They are summarized in Table 8.1.

Table 8.1.: Academic publications

Title	**Published**	**Reference**
Technology Foresight for IT Investment: Multi-Criteria Decision-Making versus Prediction Markets	AIM 2007	[118]
Preparing a Negotiated R&D Portfolio with a Prediction Market	HICSS 2008	[55]
Prediction Markets As an Innovative Way to Manage R&D Portfolios	DC CAISE 2008	[52]
Comparison of Multi-criteria and Prediction Market Approaches for Technology Foresight	AIM 2008	[54]

We also communicated our results to various management-oriented audiences, in the form of publications in newspapers and magazines, radio programs and public talks. These communications are summarized in Table 8.2.

Table 8.2.: General public communications

Title	Published	Reference
Marmix, le site qui lit l'avenir dans les marchés financiers	24 Heures (Newspaper)	[131]
Les sondages sont-ils fiables?	RSR (National Broadcast)	[40]
Mieux que les astrologues, les économistes voient déjà 2007	Allez-Savoir (Magazine)	[24]
La Bourse s'invite au Palais fédéral	Le Matin (Newspaper)	[56]
Prédire l'Avenir	Bulletin HEC (Magazine)	[51]
Météo Imprévisible	RSR (National Broadcast)	[41]
Could Science Help Predicting the Future?	UNIL (Public lecture)	[53]

8.3. An information systems design theory supporting technological forecasting

As explained in chapter 3, design work and design knowledge are important for both research and practice. Although we have already presented the contributions and communications in practice, we still need to formalize our findings as research. We chose to use Gregor and Jones's ISDT anatomy to characterize our research and our results. This section is structured according to their eight components of design theory.

8.3.1. Purpose and scope

"What the system is for", the set of meta-requirements or goals that specify the type of artifact to which the theory applies and which also defines the scope, or boundaries, of the theory

We defined the purpose of our research as being to design a prediction market to support the assessment of new technologies. More particularly, from the R&D portfolio management perspective, we studied the design factors, the underlying process and the efficiency of these markets for solving issues within this field. Our artifact supports multi-actor multi-criteria environments where data are nonexistent or difficult to collect and which do not imply extensive methodological knowledge from the stakeholders.

8.3.2. Constructs

Representations of the entities of interest in the theory

The central construct we used is the claim. It represents the subject assessed by the prediction market. We made some contributions in this context, regarding the claim's formulation, its IPO process and its settlement. Other main constructs are the traders, the market and the knowledge. Traders are players who are willing to share bits of knowledge with other traders through the market. The market is the information aggregator used by traders in order to share their knowledge about the claims. It has some properties inspired by traditional exchanges. Finally, the knowledge represents the information, private or public, available to a trader about a given claim, and the incentive for sharing it is that the trader can buy or sell, as appropriate, and then make a net gain on the basis of the price changes that occur when they release the information.

8.3.3. Principles of form and function

The abstract "blueprint" or architecture that describes an IS artifact, either product or method/intervention

In chapter 4 we described the architecture of our artifact, presenting its main functions and their implementation: (1) user account management, (2) portfolio management, (3) claims management and (4) performance measurement. Also, we developed and used a design factors typology to represents its main capabilities: (1) incentive mechanisms, (2) trading process, (3) investor management and (4) clearing house.

8.3.4. Artifact mutability

The changes in state of the artifact anticipated in the theory, that is, what degree of artifact change is encompassed by the theory

Through our design factors typology, we already support artifact mutability by providing the necessary knowledge to do it. Thus, we do not provide complete mutability rules to guarantee the behavior of the artifact after its evolution. Further work should be done in this field to support random changes in the design and to derive the necessary changes to guarantee the faultless functioning of the artifact.

8.3.5. Testable propositions

Truth statements about the design theory

We provide two categories of testable propositions. First of all, we made five general design propositions in order to design a prediction market for technological forecasting: (1) a standard framework to support claim formulation, (2) an easy IPO mechanism to support the innovation process, (3) a simplified trading interface, (4) a combination of group and individual sessions and (5) an automatic market maker. We also made specific design propositions based on our design factors typology to build a specific artifact to support the R&D portfolio management process. These propositions are summarized in Table 8.3.

8.3.6. Justificatory knowledge

The underlying knowledge or theory from the natural or social or design sciences that gives a basis and explanation for the design (kernel theories)

We made extensive use of the knowledge body to build our theory. The theories used in this research come from the prediction markets field, requirement engineering, decision support systems, technology foresight, R&D management, economics and various design-science theories. These

Table 8.3.: Main characteristics of a prediction market for R&D portfolio management

Characteristic	Design proposition
Participants	open
Claim	framework/ontology
IPO	yes (auction)
Final payout	VWAP
Market duration	open
Initial grant	cash
Trading	CDAwMM

theories were used to iteratively design, build and refine our artifact and are now parts of our construct.

8.3.7. Principles of implementation

A description of processes for implementing the theory (either product or method) in specific contexts

To support practitioners, we contributed a roadmap to implement our artifact in a real context. This roadmap should assist stakeholders to determine what the main steps are to successfully run a prediction market for technological forecasting. Moreover, through our comparison framework, we propose a decision support tool to assist stakeholders in choosing the right tool to cover their needs. Aided by these two contributions, one should be able to determine whether prediction markets are the appropriate tool for a particular context and, if so, to implement it following the roadmap provided.

8.3.8. Expository instantiation

A physical implementation of the artifact that can assist in representing the theory both as an expository device and for purposes of testing

We provide five examples of physical implementations of the artifact in different contexts. All these implementations were parts of our iterative process of building a better tool, and they were refined as a result of the evaluation process. These implementations, derived from our first MarMix prototypes, were used to test various design settings of our artifact before being refined.

8.4. Research contributions

In the introduction, we defined our research questions as being to demonstrate that specifically designed prediction markets are able to efficiently solve complex technological forecasting issues. This involves studying the design principles of these prediction markets, their adequacy for solving complex claims and their efficiency compared to other tools.

8.4.1. Adequacy

We found that prediction markets are able to solve complex issues, given that some design propositions are followed. In chapter 5 we refined our design, presenting four design experiments and showing that following five design propositions that we derived from our experiments, prediction markets are an adequate tool for solving complex technological forecasting issues.

8.4.2. Design

In chapter 4 we built and instantiated a prediction market prototype. In order to support our design process, we defined a typology of design factors to support the design of prediction markets. These design factors were successfully applied to our artifact to support various forecasting issues. Based on these results, we showed that prediction markets are able to solve some important issues of the R&D portfolio management process (chapter 6). We also designed a comparison framework for technological forecasting methods in chapter 7 to support stakeholders comparing and choosing the best forecasting method for solving issues in their particular context.

8.4.3. Efficiency

To conclude our research, we benchmarked a traditional technological foresight method (MCDM) with a prediction market (chapter 7). We found that a crowd of students was able to make the same forecasts as a selected group of experts, which seems to be counter-intuitive, even if it confirms previous results. Furthermore, we showed that in order to reach the same results, prediction markets are much more efficient than MCDM, in terms of the resources needed to set up, run and evaluate the assessments.

8.5. Final thoughts

In this research we designed an IT artifact and an approach for supporting technology foresight. We confirmed that prediction markets are adapted and perform well in predicting the emergence of new technologies. We have also shown that a design-science approach, with its iterative build-and-evaluate loops, was suitable to tackle this sort of issue. Finally, we have made some theoretical contributions that will probably be helpful for other researchers confronted with the design of innovative prediction markets, as well as for stakeholders looking at the best technological forecasting tool to implement in their organization.

For further research, we propose four possible extensions in line with our previous work.

8.5.1. Design of prediction markets applications

Currently, prediction markets and other similar DSS tools are lacking an efficient method of addressing the requirement analysis from the business point of view: the goal of the assessment. We therefore propose to develop an ontology-based method to support the design of prediction-market-based forecasting tools. This method should help managers to design their tool based on their business needs, using and sharing business ontology. Furthermore, design constraints should guarantee that the resulting application will follow the necessary requirements for addressing the final objective.

8.5.2. Generation of prediction markets shares

To better address technological foresight using prediction markets, we should be able to create the required shares based on the emergence of new technologies. We propose to use artificial intelligence methods to detect these technologies and to formalize them using ontology. More specifical, we propose to design an artifact using a classificator to extract emerging technologies from various sources. These should then be formatted as prediction market shares, using ontology-based transformations. Being able to discover these emerging topics should greatly enhance the value of prediction market usage in this context.

8.5.3. Instantiation of prediction markets as Green IS tools

Given the growing concern for sustainable development, our discipline has started a new research field named Green IS. Following Green IT, which is interested in solving hardware issues such as electrical consumption, active and passive cooling or recycling, Green IS is about the interaction between people and information systems. It would be interesting to design systems that provide enough information to support people in taking sustainable decisions. A future research could test the assumption that prediction markets would be better than other ideation methods for developing and evaluating sustainable propositions.

8.5.4. Analyze of participants' motivation

Prediction markets are at the borderline of crowdsourcing applications. In a sense, they are a typical crowdsourcing application, using a large group of unknown people to motivate them to work on a given topic, in our case a prediction, at a lower cost. But they tend to avoid remunerating participants in a traditional way, giving them the possibility of making profits on their own investments. However, as seen in section 6.5, there is still a need to uncover the players' motivations to act on these marketplaces. Thus, it would be interesting to use the recent research made to understand the motivations of people engaging in crowdsourcing activities and to translate them to prediction markets, to become better able to design their incentive mechanisms.

Bibliography

[1] Michael Abramowicz. The hidden beauty of the quadratic market scoring rule: a uniform liquitity market maker, with variations. *The Journal of Prediction Markets*, 1(2):111–125, 2007.

[2] Michael Abramowicz, Joyce E. Berg, Robin Hanson, John O. Ledyard, Thomas A. Rietz, Cass R. Sunstein, Justin Wolfers, and Eric Zitzewitz. *Information markets*. AEI Press, Washington, DC, March 2006.

[3] Bernd H. Ankenbrand and Caroline Rudzinski. Description & analysis of information markets. Witten/Herdecke University, 2005.

[4] Norm P. Archer and Fereidoun Ghasemzadeh. An integrated framework for project portfolio selection. *International Journal of Project Management*, 17(4):207–216, August 1999.

[5] Kenneth J. Arrow, Robert Forsythe, Michael Gorham, Robin Hahn, Robert; Hanson, John O. Ledyard, Saul Levmore, Robert Litan, Paul Milgrom, Forrest D. Nelson, George R. Neumann, Marco Ottaviani, Thomas C. Schelling, Robert J. Shiller, Vernon L. Smith, Cass R. Snowberg, Erik; Sunstein, Paul C. Tetlock, Philip E. Tetlock, Hal R. Varian, Justin Wolfers, and Eric Zitzewitz. The promise of prediction markets. *Science*, 320(5878):877–878, May 2008.

[6] Martin Barner, Francesco Feri, and Charles R. Plott. On the microstructure of price determination and information aggregation with sequential and asymmetric information arrival in an experimental asset market. Social Science Working Paper 1204, August 2004.

[7] Shmuel Baruch. Who benefits from an open limit order book? *The Journal of Business*, 78(4):1267–1306, July 2005.

[8] Tom W. Bell. Gambling for the good, trading for the future: The legality of markets in science claims. *Chapman Law Review*, 5:159–180, 2002.

[9] Tom W. Bell. Prediction markets for promoting the progress of science and the useful arts. *George Mason Law Review*, 14(1):37, August 2006.

[10] Tom W. Bell. Private prediction markets and the law. *The Journal of Prediction Markets*, 3(1):89–110, 2009.

[11] R Benayoun, B Roy, and B Sussmann. Manuel de référence du programme electre. Technical report, Direction scientifique SEMA, Paris, 1966.

[12] Henry Berg and Todd A. Proebsting. Hanson's automated market maker. *The Journal of Prediction Markets*, 3(1):45–59, 2009.

[13] Joyce Berg, Robert Forsythe, Forrest Nelson, and Thomas Rietz. Results from a dozen years of election futures market research, 2000.

[14] Joyce Berg, Forrest Nelson, and Thomas Rietz. Accuracy and forecast standard error of prediction markets. Tippie College of Business Administration, University of Iowa, July 2003.

[15] Joyce E. Berg, Robert Forsythe, and Thomas A. Rietz. What makes markets predict well? evidence from the iowa electronic markets. In Albers W, Güth W, Hammerstein P, Moldovanu B, and van Damme E, editors, *Understanding strategic interaction: Essays in honor of Reinhard Selten*, pages 444–463. Springer, New York, 1996.

[16] Joyce E. Berg, Robert Forsythe, and Thomas A. Rietz. The iowa electronic market. In Dean Paxson and Douglas Wood, editors, *Blackwell Encyclopedic Dictionary of Finance*, pages 111–113. Blackwell, Oxford UK, 1997.

[17] Joyce E. Berg, George R. Neumann, and Thomas A. Rietz. Searching for google's value: Using prediction markets to forecast market capitalization prior to an initial public offering. *Management Science*, 55(3):348–361, 2009.

[18] Joyce E. Berg and Thomas A. Rietz. Longshots, overconfidence and efficiency on the iowa electronic market. Working Paper, 2002.

[19] Joyce E. Berg and Thomas A. Rietz. Prediction markets as decision support systems. *Information Systems Frontiers*, 5(1):79–93, 2003.

[20] Joyce E. Berg and Thomas A. Rietz. The iowa electronic markets: Stylized facts and open issues. In Robert W. Hahn and Paul C. Tetlock, editors, *Information Markets: A New Way of Making Decisions*, pages 142–169. AEI Press, Washington D.C., 2006.

[21] Ole Jakob Bergfjord. Prediction markets as a tool for management of political risk. *The Journal of Prediction Markets*, 2(2):1–12, 2008.

[22] William R. Bitman and Nawaz Sharif. A conceptual framework for ranking r&d projects. *IEEE Transactions on Engineering Management*, 55(2):267–278, May 2008.

[23] Richard Borghesi. Price biases in a prediction market: Nfl contracts on tradesports. *The Journal of Prediction Markets*, 1(3):233–253, 2007.

[24] Geneviève Brunet. Mieux que les astrologues, les économistes voient déjà 2007. Allez Savoir, October 2007.

[25] Tung Bui. Building effective multiple criteria decision models: A decision support system approach. *Systems, Objectives, Solutions*, 4(1):3–16, 1984.

[26] Tung X. Bui. *Co-oP: A Group Decision Support System for Cooperative Multiple Criteria Group Decision Making*, volume 290 of *Lecture Notes in Computer Science*. Springer, 1987.

[27] Nicholas Chan, Ely Dahan, Adlar Kim, Andrew Lo, and Tomaso Poggio. Securities trading of concepts. Center for eBusiness @ MIT - Paper 172, July 2008.

[28] Kay-Yut Chen, Leslie R. Fine, and Bernardo A. Huberman. Forecasting uncertain events with small groups. In *Proceedings of the 3rd ACM conference on Electronic Commerce*, pages 58–64, Tampa, Florida, USA, 2001. ACM.

[29] Kay-Yut Chen, Leslie R. Fine, and Bernardo A. Huberman. Predicting the future. *Information Systems Frontiers*, 5(1):47–61, 2003.

[30] Yiling Chen, Tracy Mullen, and Chao-Hsien Chu. An in-depth analysis of information markets with aggregate uncertainty. *Electronic Commerce Research*, 6(2):201–221, 2006.

[31] Yiling Chen, David M. Pennock, and Tejaswi Kasturi. An empirical study of dynamic pari-mutuel markets: Evidence from the tech buzz game. In *Proceedings of the Web Mining and Web Usage Analysis workshop (WebDKK)*, Las Vegas, Nevada, August 24-27 2008.

[32] C. F. Chien. A portfolio-evaluation framework for selecting r&d projects. *R and D Management*, 32(4):359–368, 2002.

[33] Jed D. Christiansen. Prediction markets: Practical experiments in small markets and behaviours observed. *The Journal of Prediction Markets*, 1(1):17–41, 2007.

[34] Terry Connolly, Leonard M. Jessup, and Joseph S. Valacich. Effects of anonymity and evaluative tone on idea generation in computer-mediated groups. *Management Science*, 36(6):689–703, June 1990.

[35] Robert G. Cooper, Scott J. Edgett, and Elko J. Kleinschmidt. New product portfolio management: practices and performance. *Journal of Product Innovation Management*, 16(4):333–351, July 1999.

[36] Robert G. Cooper, Scott J. Edgett, and Elko J. Kleinschmidt. *Portfolio Management for New Products*. Perseus Books, 2nd edition, 2001.

[37] B. Cowgill, J. Wolfers, and E. Zitzewitz. Using prediction markets to track information flows: Evidence from google. Working paper, Google, January 2008.

[38] Ely Dahan, Arina Soukhoroukova, and Martin Spann. New product development 2.0: Preference markets. how scalable securities markets identify winning product concepts & attributes. *Journal of Product Innovation Management*, forthcoming, 2010.

[39] Ely Dahan and V Srinivasan. The predictive power of internet-based product concept testing using visual depiction and animation. *Journal of Product Innovation Management*, 17(2):99–109, September 2000.

[40] Fathi Derder. Les sondages sont-ils fiables? Le Grand 8, RSR La Première, September 2006.

[41] Fathi Derder. Météo imprévisible. Le Grand 8, RSR La Première, May 2008.

[42] Bruno Deschamps and Olivier Gergaud. Efficiency in betting markets: Evidence from english football. *The Journal of Prediction Markets*, 1(1):61–73, 2007.

[43] D. Harold Doty and William H. Glick. Typologies as a unique form of theory building: Toward improved understanding and modeling. *Academy of Management Review*, 19(2):230–251, April 1994.

[44] Matthew Einbinder. Information markets: Using market predictions to make today's decisions. *Virginia Law Review*, 92(1):149–186, 2006.

[45] Eugene F. Fama. Efficient capital markets: A review of theory and empirical work. *The Journal of Finance*, 25(2):383–417, May 1970.

[46] Joan Feigenbaum, Lance Fortnow, David M. Pennock, and Rahul Sami. Computation in a distributed information market. *Theoretical Computer Science*, 343(1-2):114–132, 2005.

[47] Peter C. Fishburn. Additive utilities with incomplete product sets: Application to priorities and assignments. *Operations Research*, 15(3):537–542, May-Jun 1967.

[48] Robert Forsythe, Forrest Nelson, George R. Neumann, and Jack Wright. Anatomy of an experimental political stock market. *American Economic Review*, 82(5):1142–1161, 1992.

[49] Bruno S. Frey and Felix Oberholzer-Gee. The cost of price incentives: An empirical analysis of motivation crowding-out. *The American Economic Review*, 87(4):746–755, September 1997.

[50] Cédric Gaspoz. Utilisation d'un marché de prédictions dans le cadre du projet mics. Master's thesis, Faculty of Business and Economics, University of Lausanne, 2005.

[51] Cédric Gaspoz. Prédire l'avenir. Bulletin HEC, November 2007.

[52] Cédric Gaspoz. Prediction markets as an innovative way to manage r&d portfolios. In *Proceedings of the 15th Doctoral Consortium at CAiSE-2008*, pages 62–73, Montpellier, France, June 16-17 2008. CAISE.

[53] Cédric Gaspoz. Could science help predicting the future? Public lecture, University of Lausanne, March 2009.

[54] Cédric Gaspoz, Jan Ondrus, and Yves Pigneur. Comparison of multi-criteria and prediction market approaches for technology foresight. In *Proceedings of the 13th Conference of the Association Information and Management (AIM)*, Paris, France, December 14 2008. AIM.

[55] Cédric Gaspoz and Yves Pigneur. Preparing a negotiated r&d portfolio with a prediction market. In *Proceedings of the 41st Hawaii International Conference on System Science (HICSS-41)*, page 10, Hawaii, January 2008. IEEE Computer Society.

[56] Stéphanie Germanier. La bourse s'invite au palais fédéral. Le Matin Dimanche, August 2007.

[57] Steven Gjerstad. Risk aversion, beliefs, and prediction market equilibrium. Economic Science Laboratory, University of Arizona, January 2005.

[58] Andreas Graefe and Christof Weinhardt. Long-term forecasting with prediction markets a field experiment on applicability and expert confidence. *The Journal of Prediction Markets*, 2(2):71–91, 2008.

[59] Shirley Gregor. The nature of theory in information systems. *Management Information Systems Quarterly*, 30(3):611–642, 2006.

[60] Shirley Gregor and David Jones. The anatomy of a design theory. *Journal of the Association for Information Systems*, 8(5):312–335, 2007.

[61] M J Gregory. Technology management: a process approach. *Proceedings of the Institution of Mechanical Engineers*, 209(52):347–356, June 1995.

[62] Thomas S. Gruca. The iem movie box office market: Integrating marketing and finance using electronic markets. *Journal of Marketing Education*, 22(1):5–14, 2000.

[63] Thomas S. Gruca and Joyce E. Berg. Public information bias and prediction market accuracy. *The Journal of Prediction Markets*, 1(3):219–231, 2007.

[64] Thomas S. Gruca, Joyce E. Berg, and Michael Cipriano. Do electronic markets improve forecasts of new product success? University of Iowa Working paper, June 2001.

[65] Thomas S. Gruca, Joyce E. Berg, and Michael Cipriano. The effect of electronic markets on forecasts of new product success. *Information Systems Frontiers*, 5(1):95–105, January 2003. The Effect of Electronic Markets on Forecasts of New Product Success.

[66] Thomas S. Gruca, Joyce E. Berg, and Cipriano Michael. Incentive and accuracy issues in movie prediction markets. *The Journal of Prediction Markets*, 2(1):29–43, 2008.

[67] Robert W. Hahn and Paul C. Tetlock. Using information markets to improve public decision making. *Harvard Journal of Law & Public Policy*, 29(1):214–289, Fall 2005.

[68] Robert W. Hahn and Paul C. Tetlock. Introduction to information markets. In Robert W. Hahn and Paul C. Tetlock, editors, *Information Markets: A New Way of Making Decisions*, pages 1–12. AEI Press, Washington D.C., 2006.

[69] Robert W. Hahn and Paul C. Tetlock. A new approach for regulating information markets. *Journal of Regulatory Economics*, 29(3):265–281, 2006.

[70] Robert W. Hahn and Paul C. Tetlock. A new tool for promoting economic development. In Robert W. Hahn and Paul C. Tetlock, editors, *Information Markets: A New Way of Making Decisions*, pages 170–194. AEI Press, Washington D.C., 2006.

[71] R Hanson. Book orders for market scoring rules. George Mason University, April 2003.

[72] Robin Hanson. Idea futures: Encouraging an honest consensus. *Extropy*, 3(2):7–17, 1992.

[73] Robin Hanson. Could gambling save science? encouraging an honest consensus. *Social Epistemology: A Journal of Knowledge, Culture and Policy*, 9(1):3–33, 1995.

[74] Robin Hanson. Decision markets. *IEEE Intelligent Systems*, 14(3):16–20, May/June 1999.

[75] Robin Hanson. Combinatorial information market design. *Information Systems Frontiers*, 5(1):107–119, January 2003.

[76] Robin Hanson. Decision markets for policy advice. In Eric Patashnik and Alan Gerber, editors, *Promoting the General Welfare: American Democracy and the Political Economy of Government Performance*. Brookings Institution Press, Washington D.C., September 2006.

[77] Robin Hanson. Designing real terrorism futures. *Public Choice*, 128(1):257–274, July 2006.

[78] Robin Hanson. Foul play in information markets. In Robert W. Hahn and Paul C. Tetlock, editors, *Information Markets: A New Way of Making Decisions*, pages 126–141. AEI Press, Washington D.C., 2006.

[79] Robin Hanson. Impolite innovation: The technology and politics of 'terrorism futures' and other decision markets. In Eric Patashnik and Alan Gerber, editors, *Promoting the General Welfare: American Democracy and the Political Economy of Government Performance*. Brookings Institution Press, Washington D.C., 2006.

[80] Robin Hanson. Logarithmic market scoring rules for modular combinatorial information aggregation. *The Journal of Prediction Markets*, 1(1):3–15, 2007.

[81] Robin Hanson. On market maker functions. *The Journal of Prediction Markets*, 3(1):61–63, 2009.

[82] Robin Hanson and Ryan Oprea. Manipulators increase information market accuracy. DIMACS Workshop on Markets as Predictive Devices, July 2004.

[83] FA Hayek. The use of knowledge in society. *American Economic Review*, 35(4):519–530, 1945.

[84] Alan R. Hevner, Salvatore T. March, Jinsoo Park, and Sudha Ram. Design science in information systems research. *Management Information Systems Quarterly*, 28(1):75–106, March 2004.

[85] Jeevan Jaisingh, Shailendra Mehta, and Alok Chaturvedi. An experimental study of information markets. In *Proceedings of The 7th INFORMS Conference on Information Systems and Technology*, San Jose, California, USA, 2002.

[86] Duncan James and R. Mark Isaac. Asset markets: How they are affected by tournament incentives for individuals. *The American Economic Review*, 90(4):995–1004, Sep 2000.

[87] Leonard M. Jessup, Terry Connolly, and Jolene Galegher. The effects of anonymity on gdss group process with an idea-generating task. *MIS Quarterly*, 14(3):313–321, September 1990.

[88] Ajit Kambil. Leading with an invisible hand. Outlook Journal, July 2002.

[89] Ajit Kambil and Eric van Heck. Reengineering the dutch flower auctions: A framework for analyzing exchange organizations. *INFORMATION SYSTEMS RESEARCH*, 9(1):1–19, March 1998.

[90] Gregory E. Kersten. *Multicriteria Analysis*, chapter Support for Group Decisions and Negotiations. An Overview., pages 332–346. Springer, 1997.

[91] Ken Kittlitz. Experiences with the foresight exchange. *Extropy: Journal of Transhumanist Solutions*, 06, 1999.

[92] Erica Klarreich. Best guess. *Science News*, 164(16):251–253, October, 18 2003.

[93] HK Klein and MD Myers. A set of principles for conducting and evaluating interpretive field studies in information systems. *MIS quarterly*, pages 67–93, 1999.

[94] Alexander K. Koch and Hui-Fai Shing. Bookmaker and pari-mutuel betting: Is a (reverse) favourite-longshot bias built-in? *The Journal of Prediction Markets*, 2(2):29–50, 2008.

[95] W Kuechler and V Vaishnavi. The emergence of design research in information systems in north america. *Journal of Design Research*, 7(1):1–16, 2008.

[96] Christina LaComb, Janet Barnett, and Qimei Pan. The imagination market. *Information Systems Frontiers*, 9(2):245–256, July 2007.

[97] Christina LaComb, Janet Barnett, and Qimei Pan. Designing information markets. Technical Report 2008GRC717, GE Global Research, Computational Intelligence Laboratory, Niskayuna, October 2008.

[98] Jim Lavoie. The innovation engine at rite-solutions: Lessons from the ceo. *The Journal of Prediction Markets*, 3(1):1–11, 2009.

[99] John Ledyard, Robin Hanson, and Takashi Ishikida. An experimental test of combinatorial information markets. *Journal of Economic Behavior & Organization*, 69(2):182–189, February 2009.

[100] John O. Ledyard. Designing information markets for policy analysis. In Robert W. Hahn and Paul C. Tetlock, editors, *Information Markets: A New Way of Making Decisions*, pages 37–66. AEI Press, Washington D.C., 2006.

[101] Reuven R. Levary and Dongchui Han. Choosing a technological forecasting method. *Industrial Management*, 37(1):14—18, Jan/Feb 1995.

[102] Matthew J. Liberatore and George J. Titus. The practice of management science in r&d project management. *Management Science*, 29(8):962–974, August 1983.

[103] E. Lichtenthaler. Technology intelligence processes in leading european and north american multinationals. *R & D Management*, 34(2):121–135, March 2004.

[104] E. Lichtenthaler. The choice of technology intelligence methods in multinationals: towards a contingency approach. *International Journal of Technology Management*, 32(3-4):388–407, 2005.

[105] Robert E. Litan. Comment on bell article. *The Journal of Prediction Markets*, 3(1):111–112, 2009.

[106] Shantha Liyanage, Paul F. Greenfield, and Robert Don. Towards a fourth generation r&d management model-research networks in knowledge management. *International Journal of Technology Management*, 18(3-4):372–393, July 2003.

[107] Stefan Luckner. How to pay traders in information markets: Results from a field experiment. *The Journal of Prediction Markets*, 1(2):147–156, 2007.

[108] Stefan Luckner. Prediction markets: Fundamentals, key design elements, and applications. In *Proceedings of the 21st Bled eConference*, Bled, Slovenia, June 15-18 2008.

[109] TW Malone. Bringing the market inside. *Harvard business review*, 82(4):106, 04 2004.

[110] Michael T. Maloney and J. Harold Mulherin. The complexity of price discovery in an efficient market: the stock market reaction to the challenger crash. *Journal of Corporate Finance*, 9(4):453–479, September 2003.

[111] Bernard Mangold, Mike Dooley, Rael Dornfest, Gary W. Flake, Havi Hoffman, Tejaswi Kasturi, and David M. Pennock. The tech buzz game. *IEEE Computer*, 38(7):94–97, 2005.

[112] Charles F. Manski. Interpreting the predictions of prediction markets. *Economic Letters*, 91(3):425–429, June 2006.

[113] ST March and GF Smith. Design and natural science research on information technology. *Decision Support Systems*, 15(4):251–266, 1995.

[114] Joseph P. Martino. A review of selected recent advances in technological forecasting. *Technological Forecasting and Social Change*, 70(8):719–733, October 2003.

[115] JD McKeen and H Smith. *Making IT happen: critical issues in IT management*. Wiley, 2003.

[116] Markus Noeth, Colin F. Camerer, Charles R. Plott, and Martin Weber. Information aggregation in experimental asset markets: Traps and misaligned beliefs. California Institute of Technology, Working Papers 1060, August 1999.

[117] JF Nunamaker and M Chen. Systems development in information systems research. In *Proceedings of the Twenty-Third Annual Hawaii International Conference on System Sciences*, volume 3, 1990.

[118] Jan Ondrus, Cédric Gaspoz, and Yves Pigneur. Technology foresight for it investment: Multi-criteria decision-making versus prediction markets. In *Proceedings of the 6th French affiliated AIM pre-ICIS workshop*, page 4, Montreal, Canada, December 2007.

[119] Jan Ondrus, Jean-Sébastien Monzani, and Yves Pigneur. A gdss for visualizing and assessing a technology environment. In *Proceedings of the 12th Americas Conference on Information Systems (AMCIS)*, page 209, 2006.

[120] Jan Ondrus and Yves Pigneur. Cross-industry preferences for development of mobile payments in switzerland. *Electronic Markets*, 17(2):142–152, June 2007.

[121] Jan Ondrus and Yves Pigneur. Near field communication: an assessment for future payment systems. *Information Systems and E-Business Management*, 7(3):347–361, June 2009.

[122] Gerhard Ortner. Forecasting markets - an industrial application, part i. TU Vienna, Dep. of Managerial Economics and Industrial Organization, July 1997.

[123] Gerhard Ortner. Forecasting markets - an industrial application, part ii. TU Vienna, Dep. of Managerial Economics and Industrial Organization, 1998.

[124] Marco Ottaviani and Peter Norman Sorensen. Aggregation of information and beliefs in prediction markets. London Conference on Information and Prediction Markets, May 2007.

[125] Ken Peffers, Tuure Tuunanen, Marcus Rothenberger, and Samir Chatterjee. A design science research methodology for information systems research. *Journal of Management Information Systems*, 24(3):45–77, 2008.

[126] David M. Pennock. A dynamic pari-mutuel market for hedging, wagering, and information aggregation. In *Proceedings of the 5th ACM conference on Electronic commerce*, pages 170–179, New York, NY, USA, 2004.

[127] David M. Pennock, Sandip Debnath, Eric J. Glover, and C. Lee Giles. Modeling information incorporation in markets, with application to detecting and explaining events. In *Proceedings of the Eighteenth Conference on Uncertainty in Artificial Intelligence*, pages 405–413, Alberta, Canada, 2002.

[128] David M. Pennock, Steve Lawrence, C. Lee Giles, and Finn Arup Nielsen. The power of play: Efficiency and forecast accuracy in web market games. NEC Research Institute Technical Report 2000-168, February 2001.

[129] David M. Pennock, Steve Lawrence, C. Lee Giles, and Finn Arup Nielsen. The real power of artificial markets. *Science*, 291(5506):987–988, February 2001.

[130] Jacques Pictet and Dominique Bollinger. *Adjuger un marché au mieux-disant. analyse multicritère, pratique et droit des marchés publics*. Presses polytechniques et universitaires romandes, Lausanne, 2003.

[131] François Pilet. Marmix, le site qui lit l'avenir dans les marchés financiers. 24 Heures, December 5 2005.

[132] Charles R. Plott. Markets as information gathering tools. *Southern Economic Journal*, 67(1):2–15, July 2000.

[133] Charles R. Plott and Kay-Yut Chen. Information aggregation mechanisms: Concept, design and implementation for a sales forecasting problem. California Institute of Technology, Working Papers 1131, 2002.

[134] Charles Polk, Robin Hanson, John Ledyard, and Takashi Ishikida. The policy analysis market: an electronic commerce application of a combinatorial information market. In *Proceedings of the 4th ACM conference on Electronic commerce*, pages 272–273, San Diego, CA, USA, 2003. ACM Press.

[135] A. L. Porter, W. B. Ashton, G. Clar, J. F. Coates, K. Cuhls, S. W. Cunningham, K. Ducatel, P. van der Duin, S. W. Cunningham, K. Ducatel, P. van der Duin, L. Georgehiou, T. Gordon, H. Linstone, V. Marchau, G. Massari, I. Miles, M. Mogee, A. Salo, F. Scapolo, R. Smits, W. Thissen, and Technology Futures Anal Me. Technology futures analysis: Toward integration of the field and new methods. *Technological Forecasting and Social Change*, 71(3):287–303, January 2004.

[136] J Pries-Heje, R Baskerville, and J Venable. Strategies for design science research evaluation. In *Proceedings of the 16th European Conference on Information Systems, Galway, Ireland*, pages 255–266, 2008.

[137] Russ Ray. Terrorism futures: a viable decision-market tool. *Futures Research Quarterly*, 20(2):31–39, 2004.

[138] Paul W. Rhode and Koleman S. Strumpf. Manipulating political stock markets: A field experiment and a century of observational data. University of Arizona, January 2007.

[139] Jeffrey A. Roberts, Il-Horn Hann, and Sandra A. Slaughter. Understanding the motivations, participation, and performance of open source software developers: A longitudinal study of the apache projects. *Management Science*, 52(7):984–999, 2006.

[140] E. S. Rosenbloom and William Notz. Statistical tests of real-money versus play-money prediction markets. *Electronic Markets*, 16(1):63–69, February 2006.

[141] Caroline Rudzinski. Informationsmärkte: Der unterschied, der einen unterschied macht. *Revue für postheroisches Management*, 4:90–95, March 2009.

[142] Ahti Salo, Tommi Gustafsson, and Ramakrishnan Ramanathan. Multicriteria methods for technology foresight. *Journal of Forecasting*, 22(2-3):235–255, March 2003.

[143] P. Savioz, A. Heer, and H. P. Tschirky. Implementing a technology intelligence system: key issues. *International Conference on Management of Engineering and Technology PICMET'01*, 1:198–199, August 2001.

[144] Thomas Seemann, Harald Hungenberg, and Enders Albrecht. The effect of stock endowments on the liquidity of prediction markets. *The Journal of Prediction Markets*, 2(3):33–46, 2008.

[145] Emile Servan-Schreiber. *Collective Wisdom*, chapter Prediction Markets: Trading Uncertainty for Collective Wisdom, page 17. 2009.

[146] Emile Servan-Schreiber, Justin Wolfers, David M. Pennock, and Brian Galebach. Prediction markets: Does money matter? *Electronic Markets*, 14(3):243–251, September 2004.

[147] Adam Siegel. Inkling: One prediction market platform provider's experience. *The Journal of Prediction Markets*, 3(1):65–85, 2009.

[148] HA Simon. *The sciences of the artificial.* MIT Press, Cambridge, 3rd edition, 1996.

[149] Herbert A. Simon. A behavioral model of rational choice. *The Quarterly Journal of Economics*, 69(1):99–118, February 1955.

[150] Jean Simos. *Evaluer l'impact sur l'environnement.* Presses polytechniques et universitaires romandes, Lausanne, 1990.

[151] Christian Slamka, Arina Soukhoroukova, and Spann Martin. Event studies in real- and play-money prediction markets. *The Journal of Prediction Markets*, 2(2):53–70, 2008.

[152] Michael A. Smith, David Paton, and Leighton Vaughan Williams. Market efficiency in person-to-person betting. *Economica*, 73(292):673–689, April 2005.

[153] Eric Snowberg, Justin Wolfers, and Eric Zitzewitz. Information (in)efficiency in prediction markets. In Leighton Vaughan Williams, editor, *Information Efficiency in Financial and Betting Markets.* Cambridge University Press, Cambridge, UK, 2005.

[154] A Soukhoroukova, Martin Spann, and Bernd Skiera. Creating and evaluating new product ideas with idea markets. In *Proceedings of AMA's 18th Annual Advanced Research Techniques Forum (A/R/T Forum)*, Sante Fe, New Mexico, 2007.

[155] Arina Soukhoroukova and Martin Spann. New product development with internet-based information markets: Theory and empirical application. In *Proceedings of the Thirteenth European Conference on Information Systems*, pages 1446–1457, Regensburg, Germany, 2005.

[156] Martin Spann and Bernd Skiera. Internet-based virtual stock markets for business forecasting. *Management Science*, 49(10):1310–1326, October 2003.

[157] Brian Spears, Christina LaComb, Interrante John, and Barnett Janet; Senturk-Dogonaksoy Deniz. Examining trader behavior in idea markets: An implementation of ge's imagination markets. *The Journal of Prediction Markets*, 3(1):17–39, 2009.

[158] Hans R. Stoll. Electronic trading in stock markets. *The Journal of Economic Perspectives*, 20(1):153–174, Winter 2006.

[159] C. Stummer and K. Heidenberger. Interactive r&d portfolio analysis with project interdependencies and time profiles of multiple objectives. *Ieee Transactions on Engineering Management*, 50(2):175–183, May 2003.

[160] Cass R. Sunstein. Group judgements: Statistical means, deliberation, and information markets. *New York University Law Review*, 80(3):962–1049, April 2004.

[161] Cass R. Sunstein. Deliberation and information markets. In Robert W. Hahn and Paul C. Tetlock, editors, *Information Markets: A New Way of Making Decisions*, pages 67–100. AEI Press, Washington D.C., 2006.

[162] Paul C. Tetlock. How efficient are information markets? evidence from an online exchange. Working Paper, 2004.

[163] Paul C. Tetlock, Robert Hahn, and Donald Lien. Designing information markets for decision making. AEI-Brookings Joint Center Working Paper No. 05-23, December 2005.

[164] Richard M. Titmuss. *The gift relationship: from human blood to social policy*. London School of Economics and Political Science, 2nd edition edition, 1997.

[165] Georgios Tziralis and Ilias Tatsiopoulos. Prediction markets: An extended literature review. *The Journal of Prediction Markets*, 1(1):75–91, 2007.

[166] V. Vaishnavi and W. Kuechler. Design research in information systems. http://www.isworld.org/Researchdesign/drisISworld.htm, January 2004.

[167] Joseph G. Walls, George R. Widmeyer, and Omar A. El Sawy. Building an information system design theory for vigilant eis. *Information Systems Research*, 3(1):36–59, 1992.

[168] R. Want. An introduction to rfid technology. *Pervasive Computing, IEEE*, 5(1):25–33, Jan.-March 2006.

[169] R Weber. Toward a theory of artifacts: A paradigmatic base for information systems research. *Journal of Information Systems*, 1(2):3–19, 1987.

[170] Brett D. Weigle. Prediction markets another tool in the intelligence kitbag. U.S. Army War College, March 2007.

[171] Justin Wolfers and Eric Zitzewitz. Prediction markets. *Journal of Economic Perspectives*, 18(2):107–126, Spring 2004.

[172] Justin Wolfers and Eric Zitzewitz. Five open questions about prediction markets. In Robert W. Hahn and Paul C. Tetlock, editors, *Information Markets: A New Way of Making Decisions*, pages 13–36. AEI Press, Washington D.C., 2006.

[173] Justin Wolfers and Eric Zitzewitz. Interpreting prediction market prices as probabilities. IZA Discussion Paper No. 2092, April 2006.

[174] Justin Wolfers and Eric Zitzewitz. Prediction markets in theory and practice. In Steven Durlauf and Lawrence Blume, editors, *The New Palgrave Dictionary of Economics*, page Forthcoming. McMillan, February 2006.

[175] Justin Wolfers and Eric Zitzewitz. Using markets to inform policy: The case of the iraq war. *Economica*, 76(32):225–250, April 2009.

[176] Shih-Wei Wu, Johnnie E.V. Johnson, and Sung Ming-Chien. Overconfidence in judgements: the evidence, the implications and the limitations. *The Journal of Prediction Markets*, 2(1):73–90, 2008.

Made in the USA
Monee, IL
01 November 2025

33469833R00138